# SPORTS
# DEVOTIONS
## FOR KIDS

WHAT THE GAMES WE LOVE

# SPORTS DEVOTIONS FOR KIDS

TEACH US ABOUT GOD & LIFE

## TRACY M. SUMNER

BARBOUR **kidz**

A Division of Barbour Publishing

Previously released as *Wild Words of Sport: 90 Devotions for Kids*

© 2019 by Barbour Publishing, Inc.

ISBN 978-1-63609-899-9

Published by Barbour Publishing, Inc., 1810 Barbour Drive, Uhrichsville, Ohio 44683, www.barbourbooks.com

*Our mission is to inspire the world with the life-changing message of the Bible.*

Member of the
Evangelical Christian
Publishers Association

Printed in the United States of America.

002139 0724 BP

# CONTENTS

# INTRODUCTION

So, what's your favorite sport? Or do you love them all?

Maybe you prefer baseball, known as "America's pastime," since it's been popular for more than 150 years. Perhaps your game is football, the United States' biggest spectator sport for the past few decades. Or maybe you're interested in soccer, hockey, bicycling, or lacrosse—the opportunities to play and watch sports, it seems, are endless.

The games all have different rules and equipment, but some things are true of every sporting event: each one has passionate fans who speak their own special language—what we're calling the "wild words of sport." In this book, you'll most likely find some terms from your favorite competition, and you'll probably learn some new ones from other sports.

We've highlighted ninety wild words or phrases—for example, *yakker, peloton, funny car, alley-oop, redshirt, goofy foot*—and explained what they mean, where they come from, or why people say them. And we've used these wild words to turn our thoughts to some really important words you'll find in the Bible.

These short devotions celebrate the games we love, the words we speak, and the God we serve. Read on to learn more about each—we think that's a slam dunk.

The Editors

# FAN

If you're like most people, you're probably a fan of something—a musical group, a movie actor, or a sports team or athlete.

The word *fan* (as it's used in sports) is actually a short form of "fanatic." If you look up that word in the dictionary, you'll find a fanatic is someone who is extremely dedicated to something or someone. Sometimes, fanatics grow so fond of their favorites that they can't see *anything* wrong with them.

Sounds like a lot of sports fans, doesn't it? You know, there's nothing wrong with admiring an athlete who is really good at a sport you enjoy. But it's wise to remember that athletes are just people too—and they aren't always good examples for you to follow.

The only person we should always follow is Jesus. God the Father sent Him as the perfect example of how we should live. Jesus left heaven and came to earth to show us what

God is really like—and what it means to truly follow Him. He set the best example in every area of life, from respecting His parents to making time for prayer to caring for the poor and lonely. And He showed the greatest love of all when He died for us on the cross.

. . . . . . . . . . . . . . . . . . . . . . . . . . . . . . . . . . . . . . . . . . .

*The one who says he belongs to Christ should live the same kind of life Christ lived.*
1 JOHN 2:6

# CAN OF CORN

Imagine a baseball game on TV, with the announcer saying, "Here's the pitch—Martinez swings and lifts a *can of corn* into right field." Would you think, *Huh?*

There's no metal or vegetables in this "can o' corn." It's just an easily caught fly ball.

No one knows exactly how the phrase started, but some think it goes way back to the 1800s. Long before people shopped in big supermarkets, they bought their groceries in small stores. Shopkeepers would often stack their goods on tall shelves—and if someone needed a can of corn from way up high, the grocer would reach for it with a hooked stick, pull the can toward him, then catch it in his apron. People began comparing that easy catch to a soft fly ball.

Unlike certain plays in baseball, *life* is not a can of corn. Because we live in a sinful world, bad things happen—divorce, death, sickness, loneliness. Sometimes, we even suffer for doing right—the Bible calls that "persecution."

The good news is this: our troubles are no match for God. Jesus once warned His disciples about the hardships they would face, then said, "I have told you these things so you may have peace in Me. In the world you will have much trouble. But take hope! I have power over the world!" (John 16:33).

To Jesus, everything's a can of corn.

. . . . . . . . . . . . . . . . . . . . . . . . . . . . . . . . . . . . . . . . .

*I am happy to be weak and have troubles*
*so I can have Christ's power in me.*
2 CORINTHIANS 12:9

# SQUIB KICK

Please note the spelling here: "*squib* kick," not "*squid* kick." Football players aren't booting some unfortunate, multiarmed sea creature. (Speaking of which, did you know that hockey fans in Detroit have a tradition of throwing octopi onto the ice? But that's a story for another time.)

The squib is a low-level kickoff that bounces along the field. Since footballs often take funny hops, squib kicks are harder to catch and less likely to result in a long return. So coaches occasionally call for a squib rather than a high, booming kickoff.

As is often the case, the origin of the name is hard to pinpoint—but it's interesting to note that for almost 500 years, a short, humorous speech or piece of writing has been called a "squib." Funny words, funny bounces . . .funny how those things come together, isn't it?

We all like funny things, and the Bible says there is "a time to laugh" (Ecclesiastes 3:4). But when we're joking around, we should choose our words carefully. "Do not be guilty of telling bad stories and of foolish talk," the apostle Paul said. "Instead, you are to give thanks for what God has done for you" (Ephesians 5:4).

In football, a squib kick is sometimes the right call. In life, you'll never go wrong with careful, grateful speech.

. . . . . . . . . . . . . . . . . . . . . . . . . . . . . . . . . . . . . . . . . . .

*Do not let your talk sound foolish.*
*Know how to give the right answer to anyone.*
COLOSSIANS 4:6

# BASE JUMPING

BASE jumping has nothing to do with baseball. And the name doesn't indicate jumping *up* into the air, off a "base" on the ground. No, BASE jumping is parachuting (even gliding in a wing suit) down from a tall structure rather than from an airplane. *BASE* is an acronym for *B*uilding, *A*ntenna, *S*pan, *E*arth. A span is a bridge. The "Earth" part of the name would be a high cliff.

This is considered an extreme sport. It's dangerous and in many cases illegal. Many BASE jumpers have died when the equipment they trusted to carry them safely to the ground failed.

BASE jumpers take a "leap of faith"—and some people say that's what Christians do too.

Does it make sense to believe in a God you can't see and to live your life according to an old book called the Bible? Should we fear a "crash"—of being embarrassed someday to find we trusted the wrong thing?

Every Christian has questions at some point. But when the Bible explains God and His creation, describing how people went wrong (sin) and how Jesus provided the solution (salvation), it just rings true. And our faith, then, "is being sure we will get what we hope for. It is being sure of what we cannot see" (Hebrews 11:1).

Yes, being a Christian takes faith. But there's no danger in it—God will always keep you from crashing.

. . . . . . . . . . . . . . . . . . . . . . . . . . . . . . . . . . . . . . .

*"The God Who lives forever is your safe place. His arms are always under you."*
DEUTERONOMY 33:27

# FUNNY CAR

In drag racing, "funny cars" are called that because of their looks. They sort of resemble the cars you'd see on the streets, but they have tilt-up fiberglass or carbon fiber bodies, custom-built frames, and comically oversized rear tires. They are also powered by huge supercharged, fuel-injected engines.

After a funny car rockets off the starting line, it looks like a fire-breathing dragon tearing down the strip, sometimes reaching speeds of nearly 300 miles per hour. It's loud, it makes the ground shake, and it spews smoke and fire from its exhaust pipes.

That's not funny, is it? *It's awesome!*

Do you know someone—from school or church or even at home—who feels like they're left out because they're *different*? Maybe they feel like they're funny-looking, like they're too short, too heavy, too. . .whatever it may be. But we don't all have to be exactly alike—in fact, our differences are sometimes what make us awesome.

All around us, there are lots of people who feel like they don't fit in. Sometimes, all they need are a few words of encouragement to be what God wants them to be. That doesn't cost you anything except a few minutes of your time. But it could mean everything to them.

. . . . . . . . . . . . . . . . . . . . . . . . . . . . . . . . . . . . . . .

*So encourage each other and build each other up, just as you are already doing.*
1 THESSALONIANS 5:11 NLT

# ALLEY-OOP

Hardly an NBA game goes by without at least one "alley-oop" play—and usually there are several. It's an exciting play that requires one player to throw a perfect pass near the rim so a teammate can catch the ball mid-jump and lay it in or dunk it.

Many believe the term *alley-oop* comes from the French circus term *allez hop*, which acrobats or trapeze artists cried out just before making a death-defying jump. It may surprise you to know that the English form of the term was used in the National Football League before it gained popularity in the NBA. The football alley-oop was an arching pass from the quarterback to a wide receiver tall enough to outjump a smaller defensive back in the corner of the end zone.

An alley-oop play requires great teamwork to succeed. Teamwork is always important in sports, and it's necessary in real life also.

The Bible teaches that we need other people, whether that's our family, our friends, or our classmates.

As a Christian, you can't afford to be a one-on-one player. Yes, there are times when you'll need to work things out just between you and God. But He created each of us to need other people, and He's put them in our lives for His purposes. Never forget the team-mates God's given you here on earth.

. . . . . . . . . . . . . . . . . . . . . . . . . . . . . . . . . . . . . . . . . . . . .

*Two are better than one, because they have good pay for their work.*
ECCLESIASTES 4:9

# GAME-PLANNING

When you watch the NFL on Sunday, you're not just seeing a bunch of great athletes casually playing a game. No, you're seeing the result of hours and hours of practice and game-planning that each team goes through the previous week.

A big part of this game-planning is watching films and reading game reports. These give information about the other team's players, showing what they do best and in which areas they aren't quite as strong. Knowing that can help a team to shut down the opponent's stars—or at least slow them down enough to provide a better chance of winning.

The Bible tells us that we have a spiritual opponent (an enemy, in fact) who "game-plans" to defeat us—or at least slow us down as we work to grow in our faith. That opponent is the devil, and he likes finding our weaknesses so he can attack us where we aren't strong.

good news is that God game-plans too. He knows all about the devil's schemes, and He's made us a promise: as long as we stick close to Him, He'll make sure that nothing the devil tries will hurt us. Nothing will keep us from becoming the people God wants us to be.

. . . . . . . . . . . . . . . . . . . . . . . . . . . . . . . . . . . . . . . . .

*Keep awake! Watch at all times. The devil is working against you. He is walking around like a hungry lion with his mouth open. He is looking for someone to eat.*
1 PETER 5:8

# ANCHOR

Can you imagine running a race carrying a big, heavy anchor from a ship? Fortunately for track stars, this "anchor" is just something you can rely on—in this case, the last person in a relay race.

In relays, four great runners work together as a team. While every runner is important, the most important one runs the final leg, also called the "anchor leg." This runner has a job that is simple but sometimes very difficult—to protect the team's lead or to make up ground.

Many great sprinters have earned fame by running anchor legs in major competitions. In the 1964 Summer Olympics in Tokyo, a sprinter named Bob Hayes took the baton with his 4 x 100 team in fifth place but chased down and passed all four runners ahead of him to win the gold medal.

If there's one thing sprinters who run anchor legs all have in common, it's that they're *finishers*. Their teams depend on them to finish what the first three runners have started.

How about you? Are you a finisher? Can other people depend on you to do your part? Can *God* depend on you to do the things He's called you to accomplish, either as an individual or as a part of a team?

. . . . . . . . . . . . . . . . . . . . . . . . . . . . . . . . . . . . . . . . . . . .

*I have fought a good fight. I have finished the work I was to do. I have kept the faith.*
2 TIMOTHY 4:7

# BACKSCRATCHER

Some skiers prefer to stay in contact with the ground during their entire run. Others like to zoom off a ramp and fly through the air.

Sometimes, when jumpers are in the air, they'll bend their knees and force their ski tips downward. That makes the back part of the ski rise up and touch the skier's back or shoulders. They call the move a "backscratcher," and it looks really cool.

Have you ever heard the phrase "scratching someone's back"? It means doing something for others that they can't do for themselves—at least not easily. For example, if you help your friend clean the garage at his house, you've scratched his back. That's just the kind of thing friends do for one another, isn't it?

Life gives each of us opportunities to scratch someone's back. Actually, *God* gives those opportunities, and He encourages us to take them whenever we can. That is what He meant when He said, "Love your neighbor as yourself" (Mark 12:31).

Your "neighbor" is anyone you happen across in life—people next door as well as people you've never even met. In other words, *everyone*! The opportunities to help others are everywhere, every day. Whose back can you scratch today?

. . . . . . . . . . . . . . . . . . . . . . . . . . . . . . . . . . . . . . . . . . .

*We who have strong faith should help those who are weak. We should not live to please ourselves. Each of us should live to please his neighbor. This will help him grow in faith.*
ROMANS 15:1–2

# CLEAR

Soccer goalies have one main job on the field: keep the opposing team from putting the ball into the net. But even the best goalies need help from other defensive players. When the goalie is faced with players trying to score, teammates help stop the scoring threat using what is called a "clear"—as in, "clear the ball away from the goalmouth."

In a clear, a player kicks or heads the ball away from the goal, hopefully to a teammate who can start an attack in the other direction. Sometimes, though, defensive players clear the ball just to get it away from the goal, and it ends up out of bounds or in the opponent's possession.

The Bible tells us that we have a "clear" to use when the devil tries to mess with us—and he *will* try to mess with Christians. Our clear is called faith, and that means believing that God always keeps His promises—including

His pledge to keep us secure and safe in Him.

On your own, you can't fight the devil when he tries to tempt you to do something wrong. But with God on your side, believing in Him for protection and strength, you can win every time.

. . . . . . . . . . . . . . . . . . . . . . . . . . . . . . . . . . . . . . . . . .

*Most important of all, you need a covering of faith in front of you. This is to put out the fire-arrows of the devil.*
EPHESIANS 6:16

# BEAN BALL

The phrase "bean ball" might sound funny, but it's really nothing to laugh about. A bean ball, also called "chin music," is a ball the pitcher throws to intentionally hit the batter—sometimes in the head.

Major league pitchers throw very hard, so bean balls are dangerous. Batters have been seriously hurt by bean balls, and in 1920, one player died after he was hit in the head by a pitch. That's why bean balls are forbidden in the major leagues. Pitchers who try to hit batters are often ejected and fined.

Let's face it: throwing a baseball at someone's head is wrong. It can hurt a person physically, and it can lead to angry, vengeful feelings between players.

Have you ever been tempted to hurt another person through words or actions? When that happens, it's good to remember that God knows exactly what you're thinking.

Then ask yourself this question: How would *I* like it if someone did that to me?

It's never okay with God to intentionally try to hurt another person—even when you think it's deserved. But when you treat people with kindness and forgiveness, you're showing the kind of love God wants you to have for others.

. . . . . . . . . . . . . . . . . . . . . . . . . . . . . . . . . . . . . . . . . . .

*"Do to others whatever you would like them to do to you. This is the essence of all that is taught in the law and the prophets."*
MATTHEW 7:12 NLT

# BIRDIE

If you know anything about how a game of golf is scored, you know two things: the lower the score the better. . .*and* golfers really like it when they can score their games using, well, birds!

A "birdie" is a score of one under par on any single golf hole. *Par* means the number of strokes it should take an expert golfer to put the ball in the cup. So if you're golfing on a par-three hole and you put the ball in the hole in just two strokes. . .congratulations! You've just scored a birdie!

The term *birdie* dates back to 1899. In those days, the word *bird* was used as slang for something that was very good. A well-known golfer once said, "My ball. . .came to rest within six inches of the cup. I said 'That was a bird of a shot!'" One thing led to another, and *birdie* came to be used in golf scoring. Later, the scoring terms *eagle* (two under par on a particular hole) and *double eagle* (three under) became part of golf too.

Like anyone involved in competitive sports, serious golfers work hard to become excellent at what they do. As Christians, we should do the same in everything we do. But as we work to be good at something, it shouldn't just be for our own enjoyment. Instead, we should thank God and give Him the credit for everything we accomplish.

Maybe you could sing it—like a birdie.

..............................................

*Whatever you say or do, do it in the name of the Lord Jesus. Give thanks to God the Father through the Lord Jesus.*
COLOSSIANS 3:17

# BOGEY

The word *bogey* doesn't sound like anything good, does it? In the world of golf, a bogey is a score of one *over* par on an individual golf hole.

The term originated in Great Britain in the late 1800s. It comes from a popular song called "Here Comes the Bogey Man." The bogey man in the song was a mysterious figure who hid in the shadows and challenged people to catch him.

In those days, British golfers played for the "ground score" (what we call "par" today), which they compared to chasing the bogey man.

It might seem funny to think of it this way, but the Bible teaches that God has set a "ground score" or "par" for living. In the Old Testament, He gave His people lots of rules to obey in order to be right with Him. The problem was that no one could obey the Law perfectly. You might say they all had bogeys on their scorecards.

But that all changed when God sent Jesus to earth for us. Now, when we believe in Him for salvation, we are right with God, and His rules narrow down to two: "You must love the Lord your God with all your heart and with all your soul and with all your mind," and "You must love your neighbor as you love yourself" (Matthew 22:37, 39).

. . . . . . . . . . . . . . . . . . . . . . . . . . . . . . . . . . . . . . . . . . . . . .

*You obey the whole Law when you do this one thing, "Love your neighbor as you love yourself."*
GALATIANS 5:14

# BLITZ

Few things can mess up a football team's offensive attack like a blitz. A blitz is when a linebacker or defensive back joins the defensive linemen in rushing the quarterback. It works well because it's very difficult for the offensive linemen to block all those rushing defensive players.

Another term for the blitz is "red dog." That's because linebacker Don "Red Dog" Ettinger, who played at the University of Kansas and professionally for the New York Giants, invented the defensive scheme in the late 1940s. The tactic was later called the blitz, short for the German word *blitzkrieg* ("lightning war"). The Germans used this tactic in World War II, attacking with great speed and overwhelming force as they invaded neighboring countries.

The blitz is tough to handle, just like life can be. Sometimes, it feels like the world is sending one blitz after another at us. If it's not problems at home, it's hard times at school. And if it's not hard times at school, it's conflict with our closest friends.

The good news, though, is that we have Jesus as our personal protector. And even though living for Him doesn't mean we'll be trouble-free, we can always take comfort in knowing that He's bigger than even our scariest problems.

. . . . . . . . . . . . . . . . . . . . . . . . . . . . . . . . . . . . . . . . .

*"I have told you these things so you may have peace in Me. In the world you will have much trouble. But take hope! I have power over the world!"*
JOHN 16:33

# BONK

In the world of competitive bicycling, a bonk can mean the end of a cyclist's day.

"Bonking" means hitting a wall—not physically, but in the sense of being unable to go on. When cyclists bonk, it's because their bodies have run out of glycogen, the fuel they need to operate at a high level. When the bonk hits, a rider can suddenly feel weak, tired, shaky, sweaty, dizzy, or light-headed—or a combination of those things.

Competitive cyclists know that the best way to handle a bonk is to avoid it in the first place. Sure, eating some simple carbohydrates—high-sugar foods that the body processes quickly—can help get the rider back on the road. But it's always better to prepare the body *before* the ride by eating the right foods.

That's kind of the way we avoid bonking in the Christian life. We want to be prepared for the times we'll be tempted to sin or when we need to tell others about our faith in Jesus. By "eating the right food"—that is, by reading and studying the Bible—we'll be strong enough not to bonk.

Stay close to Jesus through His Word, and you'll finish the race He's given you.

. . . . . . . . . . . . . . . . . . . . . . . . . . . . . . . . . . . . . . . .

*You know that only one person gets a crown for being in a race even if many people run. You must run so you will win the crown.*
1 CORINTHIANS 9:24

# STRETCH FOUR

It wasn't long ago that nearly all NBA teams played with two guards, a center, and two forwards—a small forward and a power forward. The power forward was a big, strong player who rebounded, played defense, and shot from less than fifteen feet from the basket.

Today, though, many power forwards are what are called "stretch fours"—big guys (up to seven feet tall) who can handle the ball, drive to the basket, and shoot all the way out to the three-point line. Two of the best stretch fours playing today are Kevin Durant and Kristaps Porzingis.

The game of basketball has changed big-time in the past few decades. Some fans think that's good, but many don't like it. Most people—even a lot of Christians—aren't comfortable with change.

The Bible is filled with stories of people who had to deal with change—changes in where they lived, changes in the work they did, changes in the world around them. But they handled the change because they were confident in one thing: their God.

Change is a part of life. But even when it makes you feel afraid or uncomfortable, you can always take comfort in the fact that God loves you and will always take care of you.

Life changes, but God never will.

. . . . . . . . . . . . . . . . . . . . . . . . . . . . . . . . . . . . . . . . .

*Jesus Christ is the same yesterday*
*and today and forever.*
HEBREWS 13:8

# THROWING ROCKS

Even the most casual bowler—you know, the kind who only bowls on a random Saturday night with friends—can have a great night at the alley. That kind of bowler often doesn't throw with any kind of "hook," the curve of the ball created by spin. He just throws the ball right down the middle as hard as he can and then watches what happens.

Good bowlers will tell you that chucking the ball fast, straight at the center pin, isn't the best way to record strikes. But sometimes it works. When it does, the bowler is said to be "throwing rocks."

Even if it's not a great bowling technique, it can still be a lot of fun when you're out bowling with friends.

There are days when it seems like everything's going our way—like we're throwing rocks at the bowling alley. When that happens—at school, at home, on the basketball court or football field—enjoy it. But don't forget to stop for a moment and tell God how grateful you are for the day He's given you.

He gets a kick out of His kids "throwing rocks."

. . . . . . . . . . . . . . . . . . . . . . . . . . . . . . . . . . . . . . .

*Be full of joy all the time. Never stop praying. In everything give thanks. This is what God wants you to do because of Christ Jesus.*
1 THESSALONIANS 5:16–18

# SOUTHPAW

Now here's an interesting baseball statistic: while only one in ten people are left-handed, almost 40 percent of major league baseball pitchers are. Some of the best pitchers of all time threw with their left hand. Three of the best recent left-handers in baseball are Madison Bumgarner, Clayton Kershaw, and Chris Sale.

Left-handed pitchers are sometimes called "southpaws." That's because most major league ballparks are constructed with the outfield in the east side. Because of this, when a pitcher is on the mound facing the plate, his left arm is toward the south.

Lots of left-handers have had great success in baseball. But outside of the game, many southpaws have to make adjustments for a world that is in most ways made for right-handed people.

As a Christian, do you ever feel like this

world just wasn't made for you—like you belong somewhere else? If so, here's why: you live in what was once a perfect world, but it's polluted by sin. This broken world is not really your home. That's the bad news.

The good news is that after Jesus died on the cross to pay for people's sins, He was raised from the dead and went back to heaven. There, He's preparing a perfect place for you (John 14:3). . .and it won't matter which hand you use for throwing.

. . . . . . . . . . . . . . . . . . . . . . . . . . . . . . . . . . . . . . . . .

*But we are citizens of heaven. Christ, the One Who saves from the punishment of sin, will be coming down from heaven again. We are waiting for Him to return.*
PHILIPPIANS 3:20

# CATCHING A CRAB

When you watch rowing events during the Summer Olympics, it looks like a pretty easy sport, doesn't it? You might even think, *Hey, I can do that!* But rowing events aren't as easy or simple as they look. Rowers spend countless hours practicing for competition, getting their timing down and their endurance up.

There's nothing more important to competitive rowers than timing. If the rower places the oar in the water at the wrong time or at the wrong angle, the oar will act as a brake rather than a propeller. Rowers call this "catching a crab," and it can spell the end of a race.

A really bad crab can actually jerk the oar from the rower's hand and sometimes even pull the rower from the boat. Though experienced rowers know the danger of catching a crab, it still happens sometimes.

Rowers aren't the only ones whose mistakes—even in small things—make life difficult. Even those of us who love God and trust Jesus will occasionally "catch a crab" as we go through life.

The good news is that God is with us even when we fail. The better news is that when we come to Him with our mistakes, He'll always forgive. God puts the oar back in our hands—and sets us back in the boat—so we can continue in His way.

. . . . . . . . . . . . . . . . . . . . . . . . . . . . . . . . . . . . . . . . . . .

*The steps of a good man are led by the Lord. And He is happy in his way. When he falls, he will not be thrown down, because the Lord holds his hand.*
PSALM 37:23–24

# DEUCE

If you don't know much about tennis, the way a match is scored can be confusing. Matches are made up of points, games, and sets. A tennis player wins a match by winning the most sets, and he wins a set by winning a certain number of games. To win a game, a player must score four points—which are counted as "fifteen," "thirty," "forty," and "game." (We said it was confusing, right?)

But if the game is tied at 40-40, one of the players must score twice in a row to win, no matter how many points are ultimately played. That's why the tied game is called a *deuce*—another term for "two."

Closely matched players can play games with many deuces, and that can make for some very long contests. Some Association of Professional Tennis (ATP) matches have gone on for several hours! When that happens, the player who can best fight off fatigue has the best chance of winning.

You don't have to be a tennis player—or even a grown-up—to sometimes feel tired, burned out, and sapped of energy. But as a Christian, you have an advantage (another tennis scoring term!): you know Jesus, who has promised to reenergize you through His Holy Spirit. Then you can keep doing the things He wants you to do.

. . . . . . . . . . . . . . . . . . . . . . . . . . . . . . . . . . . . . . . . .

*"Come to Me, all of you who work and have heavy loads. I will give you rest. Follow My teachings and learn from Me. I am gentle and do not have pride. You will have rest for your souls."*
MATTHEW 11:28–29

# OWN GOAL

If you play soccer—or if you're just a fan of the game—you probably know that the worst thing that can happen to a player is to score an "own goal." That happens when someone accidently scores a goal for the *other* team.

Own goals can happen at any level of soccer, from youth leagues all the way up to the World Cup. Believe it or not, players have scored 53 own goals in the World Cup—including an amazing 12 in 2018 alone. Imagine how embarrassed these players felt when they scored an own goal at the biggest soccer tournament in the world!

Have you ever done something that just makes you want to hide in your room? We've all had situations blow up in our faces, leaving us embarrassed. That can happen even when we haven't done anything wrong—it can happen even when we have the best intentions!

When you feel embarrassed over some-thing, fight the temptation to just hide. Instead, remember that God cares when you feel sad, angry, hurt. . .or humiliated. You shouldn't try to hide from Him—you could never hide from God anyway. Instead, if you're embarrassed by something you've done, ask forgiveness. If you're upset by something done to you, ask for comfort and wisdom. Then get back out on the field and finish the game.

. . . . . . . . . . . . . . . . . . . . . . . . . . . . . . . . . . . . . . . . . .

*See, God is my Helper. The Lord is the One Who keeps my soul alive.*
PSALM 54:4

# TOMATO CAN

In boxing, a fighter who isn't as skilled as the elite boxers is sometimes called a "tomato can"—and a boxer who usually gets easy wins over that kind of opponent is a "can crusher." Promising young boxers often build up a good record against tomato cans before they move up to face better boxers.

When he steps into the ring against an elite boxer, a tomato can is a big underdog. But every once in a while, the "can" gives a much better boxer all he can handle before losing. . .or even pulls off a shocking upset. That happened in 1990, when James "Buster" Douglas, a huge underdog, knocked out world champion Mike Tyson in a bout in Tokyo, Japan.

If you read the stories of some of the Bible's great heroes, you'll see that God likes underdogs. Many of them weren't educated, powerful, or rich, yet God chose them to do great things for Him.

Do you ever feel like a "tomato can"—like you're just not a person God can use? If so, stay in the ring. You're just the kind of person God likes to use to accomplish His plans.

. . . . . . . . . . . . . . . . . . . . . . . . . . . . . . . . . . . . . . . . . . . .

*God has chosen what the world calls foolish to shame the wise. He has chosen what the world calls weak to shame what is strong. God has chosen what is weak and foolish of the world, what is hated and not known, to destroy the things the world trusts in. In that way, no man can be proud as he stands before God.*
1 CORINTHIANS 1:27–29

# OSKIE

*Offense* and *defense* are important words in almost every sport. When you're on offense, you have the ball and you're trying to score. When you're on defense, you're trying to keep the other team from scoring. In a game like basketball, the same players switch from offense to defense as possession of the ball changes. In football, offensive and defensive players are usually separate, coming into the game after a score or punt. But then there's "oskie" time.

The origin of *oskie* isn't known for sure, but it dates back to at least the late 1930s. Robert Neyland, then the head coach at the University of Tennessee, included the term in his "Seven Maxims of Football."

"Oskie" is called by defensive players when one of their teammates intercepts a pass. When defenders hear that, they know it's time to switch to offense, blocking for their teammate so he can make a good return—maybe even a game-changing "pick-six" (a touchdown).

The Bible shows a kind of oskie, an example of switching from defense to offense, and it's in a discussion of "the whole armor of God" (Ephesians 6:13–17). These verses describe the coverings God gives us to defend against the devil's attacks. But they also tell about an amazing offensive weapon that will defeat Satan every time: the Word of God, also known as the Bible.

When you read the Bible and live the way it tells you to, you'll be a winner every time!

. . . . . . . . . . . . . . . . . . . . . . . . . . . . . . . . . . . . . . .

*Put on salvation as your helmet, and take the sword of the Spirit, which is the word of God.*
EPHESIANS 6:17 NLT

# FORE!

When you're on a golf course and hear some-one call, "Fore!" you need to watch for a fast-moving ball coming your way.

The origin of the term is interesting. It comes from Scotland, the land where golf was born, and is a shortened form of *before* or *afore*. Golfers started calling "fore!" as early as the eighteenth century, borrowing the term from Scottish artillery men. They yelled it to troops on the front lines to urge them to take cover and keep their heads down.

The Bible has many "fore!" warnings for Christians, including one to pay attention to what's happening in the world. Why? So we can keep ourselves ready for Jesus' return.

We can't know exactly when Jesus will come back. But the Bible gives us signs that that amazing day is close. Here's how Jesus described it: "You will hear of wars and lots of talk about wars. . . . There will be no food for people. The earth will shake and break apart in different places. These things are the beginning of sorrows and pains" (Matthew 24:6–8).

His message is this: "You must be ready" (Matthew 24:44).

Fore!

. . . . . . . . . . . . . . . . . . . . . . . . . . . . . . . . . . . . . . . . . .

*"Because of this, watch! You do not know on what day your Lord is coming."*
MATTHEW 24:42

# BRICK

In basketball, there are missed shots and there are badly missed shots. Then there are those shots that clang off the rim so hard that the ball seems to take some orange paint with it. When a player makes a shot like that, you might hear other players or fans call out, "Brick!"

No one knows for sure who first used the word for a bad shot. But the idea of bricks in basketball has created some other funny terms. For example, a player who is known to be a poor shooter is sometimes called a "bricklayer" or "mason."

But bricks aren't limited just to bad shooters. Even the best players throw up a brick now and again. Stars like LeBron James, Stephan Curry, and James Hardin occasionally lay a brick, but they don't let one badly missed shot define them as players. When they miss a shot, they keep doing what they know they do well: shooting.

Have you ever done something that made you look bad to others—or worse, made God look bad? Maybe you even meant well and thought you were doing the right thing, but your best shot clanged off the rim, leaving you embarrassed and discouraged. When that happens, don't give up and never try again. God wants you to trust Him, ask forgiveness, and keep shooting!

......................................

*Do not have joy over me, you who hate me. When I fall, I will rise. Even though I am in darkness, the Lord will be my light.*
MICAH 7:8

# BUNKER

Even the best golfers in the world can hurt their scores by hitting the ball into what are called "hazards." Golf courses have several types of hazards. Creeks are considered hazards. So are ponds or groves of trees. And most courses have hazards called "bunkers."

A bunker is a shallow pit filled with sand. The pit usually has a raised edge. Hitting a golf ball over that edge can be very difficult because of the sand. That's why golfers do everything they can to avoid ending up in a bunker.

This life is a lot like a golf course—filled with hazards that can keep you from being the kind of person God wants you to be. These hazards are the temptations to sin, both in our actions and our thoughts. It's hard to avoid these things, but the Bible teaches that it's not impossible.

The best way to "stay out of the bunker" is to stick close to Jesus every day. That means praying regularly, especially when you feel tempted. It also means reading and studying the Bible—and then doing what it says. As Psalm 119:11 puts it, "Your Word have I hid in my heart, that I may not sin against You."

On your own, you can easily end up in a bunker. But with Jesus as your guide, you can avoid all of life's hazards.

. . . . . . . . . . . . . . . . . . . . . . . . . . . . . . . . . . . . . . . .

*A prudent person foresees danger and takes precautions. The simpleton goes blindly on and suffers the consequences.*
PROVERBS 22:3 NLT

# CAGER

It might be hard to believe it now, but some of the first basketball games, back in the early 1900s, were rough-and-tumble affairs. When the ball bounced into the stands, it belonged to the team that got to it first, and players often threw elbows and wrestled one another for possession. Sometimes spectators even joined in the melees! The competition got so rough that teams started playing their games in cages.

Well, sort of.

To make the games safer for players and fans alike, basketball courts were surrounded by wire-mesh cages. And that, sports fans, is why basketball players are still occasionally called "cagers."

But full-contact basketball wasn't the way the game was intended. In 1892, when Dr. James Naismith published the thirteen original rules, he had said, "No shouldering, holding, striking, pushing, or tripping in any way of an opponent."

Just as Naismith wanted to protect players from injury, God gives us His rules for our own good and protection. Do you want to know where to find those rules for life? They're right in the pages of God's written Word, the Bible.

. . . . . . . . . . . . . . . . . . . . . . . . . . . . . . . . . . . . . . . . . . .

*All the Holy Writings are God-given and are made alive by Him. Man is helped when he is taught God's Word. It shows what is wrong. It changes the way of a man's life. It shows him how to be right with God. It gives the man who belongs to God everything he needs to work well for Him.*
2 TIMOTHY 3:16–17

# CHICKISMS

His full name was Francis Dayle Hearn, but basketball fans know him as "Chick" Hearn, the longtime play-by-play man for the Los Angeles Lakers. Many think Chick was the greatest sports announcer of all time. He's certainly one of the most influential, as college and NBA play-callers alike use many of his catch-phrases—which are known as "Chickisms."

During his decades-long career, Chick Hearn coined colorful phrases such as "slam dunk," "charity stripe," "air ball," "finger roll," "no harm, no foul," and "ticky-tack foul." They're still in use today, even though his last broadcast was in 2001.

Chick Hearn shows how the things people say can have a big impact on others. Just as his words influenced many other broadcasters who followed him, the words *we* speak can also influence people around us—for good and for bad.

The Bible has a lot to say about our words. It tells us that we should not use bad language, say mean things to others, tell lies, or criticize people behind their backs. Instead, we should speak only those words that encourage people, building up Christians in their faith. That will show people the difference Jesus has made in our lives.

..............................................

*Watch your talk! No bad words should be coming from your mouth. Say what is good. Your words should help others grow as Christians.*
EPHESIANS 4:29

# THE BIG UGLIES

Calling a group of guys "big uglies" doesn't sound very nice, does it? But legendary college football broadcaster Keith Jackson used this phrase as a compliment. He was honoring the players who do the dirty work it takes to make a team successful—the offensive linemen.

Jackson was talking about guys who are bigger and stronger than anyone else on a team, but whose work isn't as pretty to watch as a long touchdown run or a perfectly thrown pass. "Big uglies" just do a less exciting job. The truth is Jackson didn't care whether the guys were handsome or homely.

You know who else doesn't care about people's looks? God! That's right, God doesn't judge how handsome or pretty you are. Instead, He looks at what you choose to think about, how you treat others, and whether you try to live the way He wants you to.

There's nothing wrong with dressing nicely

or getting a stylish haircut. But don't forget that it's always what's *inside* that really matters to God.

. . . . . . . . . . . . . . . . . . . . . . . . . . . . . . . . . . . . . . . . . . .

*But the Lord said to Samuel, "Do not look at the way he looks on the outside or how tall he is, because I have not chosen him. For the Lord does not look at the things man looks at. A man looks at the outside of a person, but the Lord looks at the heart."*
1 Samuel 16:7

# CHUKKER

Polo is an amazing game to watch. Two four-player teams chase a small, hard ball, trying to knock it into the opponent's goal with a wooden mallet. And all this while everyone—even the referee—is on horseback!

While most sports divide their games into quarters or halves, a polo match is made up of seven-minute playing times called "chukkers." It's not certain where the term came from.

Players must change horses (also known as "polo ponies") after each chukker. The game wears down even the best-trained horses quickly, so the short periods are intended to protect them.

Did you know that the Bible has something to say about the way we treat animals? Proverbs 12:10 tells us that one way you can know a person is right with God is that he treats his animals well. God even made a rule for how to treat animals when He told the people of Israel that they should allow their animals to rest on the Sabbath day, just like people (see Exodus 23:12).

If you have a pet to care for—a dog, a cat, a gerbil, or a goldfish—you can show your commitment to God by giving that animal the best care you can.

. . . . . . . . . . . . . . . . . . . . . . . . . . . . . . . . . . . . . . . . . .

*A man who is right with God cares for his animal, but the sinful man is hard and has no pity.*
PROVERBS 12:10

# DROPPING A DIME

You've probably heard a sportscaster on ESPN say something like this: "Westbrook had 28 points, 10 rebounds, and 12 dimes." Pretty much everyone knows about points and rebounds, but what is a *dime*? Well, that's a slang word for an assist, which is a pass that leads directly to a basket.

Some people believe the term comes from the days before cell phones, when people used pay phones. The price of a call was ten cents, and someone without change would often ask others to help. If someone "dropped a dime," he or she was making an assist.

Some basketball players like "dropping dimes" even more than they do scoring baskets—and they're really good at it. Teammates like playing with dime-droppers because they figure they'll get the ball for an easier shot. And who doesn't like easier shots?

The Bible encourages Christians to look

out for opportunities to "drop a dime" for other people—especially other believers. There are all kinds of ways you could help others, whether your friends, your mom and dad, a classmate or neighbor.

Who can you drop a dime for today?

. . . . . . . . . . . . . . . . . . . . . . . . . . . . . . . . . . . . . . .

*Because of this, we should do good to everyone. For sure, we should do good to those who belong to Christ.*
GALATIANS 6:10

# SLAM DUNK

Most everyone has heard of the basketball term *slam dunk*. It's used when a player jams the ball through the basket with such force that it can leave the backboard shaking.

The phrase is one of many invented by the famous Los Angeles Lakers broadcaster Chick Hearn, but "slam dunk" goes way beyond basketball these days. It's also used to describe a sure thing. For example: "A cold, snowy January day in Minnesota is a slam dunk!"

Here's another slam dunk: the good life we can have through Jesus.

Jesus made many promises when He was on earth. Not only did He offer eternal life after we die, He also promised His followers an amazing life here on earth: "I came so they might have life, a great full life" (John 10:10).

Very few things in this life are absolute certainties, but you can count on God to keep His promises. And when His own Son, Jesus

Christ, says something, you know He's going to make it happen—for you and for everyone else who follows Him.

A great, full life here on earth, followed by an eternal life with God in heaven. . .when you put your trust in Jesus, it's a slam dunk for sure!

. . . . . . . . . . . . . . . . . . . . . . . . . . . . . . . . . . . . . . . .

*"I tell you, anyone who hears My Word and puts his trust in Him Who sent Me has life that lasts forever. He will not be guilty. He has already passed from death into life."*
JOHN 5:24

# BLACK HOLE

It's not easy playing with a ball hog—you know, the player who doesn't give up the ball to anyone. In lacrosse (and some other sports, such as basketball) players call ball hogs "black holes."

Real black holes are mysterious areas of outer space that have such strong gravity that nothing can escape them. When a black hole sucks something in, it's never seen again.

Can you see why a lacrosse player would call a ball hog a black hole?

Let's be honest: we're talking about a selfish player. Many times, the black hole's teammates reach a point where they don't even want to pass him the ball because they know they'll never get it back.

The Bible tells us that we shouldn't be selfish—at home, at school, at church, in sports. . .anywhere. God wants us as Christians to think about other people's needs more than our own.

You'll be a good friend when you care more about what you can do for others than what you can do for yourself. And you'll please God, who has promised to take care of you when you seek Him and His will above everything else.

. . . . . . . . . . . . . . . . . . . . . . . . . . . . . . . . . . . . . . . . .

*Do not work only for your own good.*
*Think of what you can do for others.*
1 Corinthians 10:24

# COACHABILITY

Sports history includes many examples of very talented players who never lived up to their potential—because they weren't coachable. They didn't understand that they had to allow themselves to be coached, to be taught, to be told what to do, in order to achieve their greatest success.

Players who are "uncoachable" often find some success. But they're usually labeled as underachievers, players who could have gone so much farther if they'd only listened to their coaches and did what they were told.

If you're part of a sports team, be coachable. Learn the playbook, put your team ahead of yourself, do what your coach tells you—you'll find yourself free to enjoy the game and become the best player you can be.

The same thing is true of your life with Jesus. God gave you rules and advice in the Bible not to keep you from enjoying yourself but so that you could become all He wants you to be. The book of James puts it this way: "The one who keeps looking into God's perfect Law and does not forget it will do what it says and be happy as he does it. God's Word makes men free" (James 1:25).

. . . . . . . . . . . . . . . . . . . . . . . . . . . . . . . . . . . . . . . . .

*[Jesus] said to the Jews who believed,
"If you keep and obey My Word, then you
are My followers for sure. You will know the
truth and the truth will make you free."*
JOHN 8:31–32

# FLEA FLICKER

Lots of things make a football game fun to watch. They include what football fans have come to know as "trick plays."

One of the riskiest trick plays—and the most rewarding, when it works—is the "flea flicker." It originated with a legendary coach named Bob Zuppke, who led the University of Illinois team from 1913 through 1941.

In this play, the quarterback hands off the ball to the running back, who charges up toward the line. Then he turns and tosses the ball *back* to the quarterback, who throws to what he hopes is an open receiver running free downfield.

The flea flicker is risky because the ball changes hands so many times. Several things can go wrong—and sometimes they do. But when the play works, the offensive team gets a long gain, often for a touchdown.

In the Christian life, you'll sometimes

experience "flea flicker" moments. You know that God wants you to do something, but it seems risky. The great thing about serving God, though, is that even in hard, dangerous times, He promises to be with you. He will give you the courage, strength, and faith to do the good things that scare you.

When you think about it, doing what God has asked isn't risky at all—just rewarding!

. . . . . . . . . . . . . . . . . . . . . . . . . . . . . . . . . . . . . . . . .

*"The Lord is the One Who goes before you. He will be with you. He will be faithful to you and will not leave you alone. Do not be afraid or troubled."*
DEUTERONOMY 31:8

# FOSBURY FLOP

In the 1968 Summer Olympics in Mexico City, sports fans saw something they'd never seen before: a high jumper approaching his target from the side then soaring head-and-back-first over the bar. That jumper was Dick Fosbury, and his style came to be known as the "Fosbury Flop."

Before 1968, elite high jumpers used techniques such as the straddle, the Western Roll, or the scissors jump to clear the bar. But since that time, almost all high jumpers—men and women alike—use the Fosbury Flop.

To have a generation of athletes use a technique that you originated and perfected is a great honor. But to have the technique actually named after you is another thing altogether. That's an example of leaving a *legacy*—a word describing something a person does that influences others in the future.

God wants all of us as Christians to leave a

legacy—a legacy of love for and faith in Him.
Don't think you're too young to leave a legacy,
because it's not as hard as you might think.
You can leave a legacy just by showing love
to others, speaking kindly, and doing what is
right in every situation.

You can do that today, can't you?

. . . . . . . . . . . . . . . . . . . . . . . . . . . . . . . . . . . . . . . .

*Families of this time will praise*
*Your works to the families-to-come.*
*They will tell about Your powerful acts.*
PSALM 145:4

# KNUCKLEBALL

On the baseball field, knuckleball pitchers make life difficult for a lot of people. That's because knuckleballs are hard for hitters to hit, harder for the home plate umpire to call, and even harder for the catcher to catch. The reason? No one—sometimes not even the pitcher himself—knows where the ball will end up!

A well-thrown knuckler doesn't travel very fast. But because of the way the pitcher grips the ball, it doesn't spin as it leaves his hand. When a ball doesn't rotate, the air flow around the seams makes it fly in an unpredictable way. Knuckleballs seem to dance or flutter on their way to the plate, making them very hard to hit.

Maybe you've noticed that life can be like a knuckleball—impossible to predict or control. But you can always count on one thing: God. He loves you and wants what's best for you. So when you can't make sense of everything that's going on in your life, just look up! Thank God for all He's done for you, then ask Him what you should do next.

You still might not know what's coming next. But you can relax, knowing that God's got that crazy knuckleball of life under control.

. . . . . . . . . . . . . . . . . . . . . . . . . . . . . . . . . . . . . . . . .

*Do not worry. Learn to pray about*
*everything. Give thanks to God as you*
*ask Him for what you need. The peace of*
*God is much greater than the human mind*
*can understand. This peace will keep your*
*hearts and minds through Christ Jesus.*
PHILIPPIANS 4:6–7

# SIN BIN

When a hockey player breaks the rules, the referee sends him off the ice to the penalty box—also known as the "sin bin." Most of the time, players spend two minutes of game time there. But if their bad behavior was more serious, they can spend additional time in the sin bin.

Players who break the rules hurt themselves and their team. Why? Because while they're in the penalty box, they can't help their teammates. The rest of the team has to play shorthanded.

It's a lot like that when *we* do something wrong. When we commit sins, we not only hurt our relationship with God—our actions often hurt other people too. That's why God gave us His rules for living in the Bible. It's also why He made a way for us to be forgiven when we mess up and break the rules.

Jesus came to earth, died on the cross, and then was raised from the dead so that we could be released from an eternal "sin bin." When we as Christians mess up—and we all do—we can go to God and admit what we've done, knowing that He will forgive us and offer us a new start.

. . . . . . . . . . . . . . . . . . . . . . . . . . . . . . . . . . . . . . . . . . .

*If we tell Him our sins, He is faithful and we can depend on Him to forgive us of our sins. He will make our lives clean from all sin.*
1 JOHN 1:9

# FOUL

Every sport has its own rule book, and they usually include definitions of fouls. Most sports fans know there are fouls in basketball. Football has its own list of fouls too, as does soccer. Even sports like judo and sumo wrestling have fouls.

A foul is simply an unfair or improper act on the part of one or more players—and each foul usually results in some kind of penalty. For example, a foul in basketball may give free throws to the offended team. In football, a foul results in lost yardage. If the foul is severe—like intentionally trying to hurt an opponent—it may result in a player being disqualified for the remainder of a game.

In God's rule book for life, the Bible, there are behaviors that please Him and there are "fouls." Lying, stealing, gossiping, treating others poorly—there are many ways to break the rules that make our lives better. Happily for us, though, the Bible tells us what to do when we "commit a foul," so we can get back on track with God.

The Bible is a great book. Read it every day—and then make sure you do what it says!

· · · · · · · · · · · · · · · · · · · · · · · · · · · · · · · · · · · · · · · · · ·

*All Scripture is inspired by God and is useful to teach us what is true and to make us realize what is wrong in our lives. It corrects us when we are wrong and teaches us to do what is right.*
2 TIMOTHY 3:16 NLT

# SIDE STITCH

Distance runners endure countless hours of training so they can be their very best. They often have to continue their training and competitive races when they are in physical pain.

One of those pains is called a "side stitch." Runners feel them just below the rib cage during training or competitive runs. It's not a serious medical problem, but it's intense—and it can really mess up a runner's day.

When they get a side stitch, experienced runners know how to deal with the problem. But they also know it's best to *prevent* side stitches. That involves eating the right foods (in the right amounts) before a run, as well as drinking enough liquid. To a distance runner, preventing a side stitch is all about one word: *preparation.*

The Bible teaches that Christians should also be prepared. For what? Avoiding the wrong things and being ready to do right things, like sharing our faith with other people. You'll avoid a spiritual side stitch by reading your Bible, praying, and spending time with other believers.

In the race called life, God has some great things for you to do. Are you making sure you're prepared?

...............................................

*Because Noah had faith, he built a large boat for his family. God told him what was going to happen. His faith made him hear God speak and he obeyed.*

HEBREWS 11:7

# PICK AND ROLL

One of the most basic (and effective) basketball plays is the pick and roll. In this play, a player sets a screen (another word for "pick") for a teammate dribbling the ball, then moves toward the basket to receive a pass for an easy basket. Teams at all levels of basketball—from grade school to the pros—use the play.

Some NBA point guard/forward combinations are well known for using the pick and roll. Your parents might remember John Stockton and Karl Malone back in the 1990s—Malone scored a lot of points off the play, enough to become the league's second-highest scorer of all time. More recently, Stephan Curry and Draymond Green use the play successfully.

For the pick and roll to work, players need a good sense of timing. As Christians, we do too.

The Bible talks a lot about timing. But it says that God's timing isn't always what we want it to be. Often, we have to wait on Him to do what He's promised to do. But even though we get impatient, God always does the right thing at the right time.

Waiting on God is one of the most basic (and effective) plays in our game. Know that you'll never be disappointed in the end.

. . . . . . . . . . . . . . . . . . . . . . . . . . . . . . . . . . . . . . .

*But they who wait upon the Lord will get new strength. They will rise up with wings like eagles. They will run and not get tired. They will walk and not become weak.*
ISAIAH 40:31

# GOLDEN SOMBRERO

Even the greatest athletes have bad days. Whether it's in basketball, football, hockey, or any other sport, everyone has a night they'd like to forget.

Baseball has a way of keeping its players humble anyway—even the best hitters fail about 70 percent of the time. But baseball has a term for a player who has a *really* bad game at the plate: the "golden sombrero." That refers to a player who strikes out four times in one game. Even great players can go hitless in four at-bats, but to strike out all four times? Ouch!

The term got its start in the 1980s when San Diego Padres player Carmelo Martínez coined a funny variation of hockey's "hat trick," for a player who scores three goals in a game. After "golden sombrero" caught on in baseball, other—even worse—terms were created: "Platinum Sombrero" (five strikeouts in a game) and "Titanium Sombrero" (six strikeouts).

Everybody has bad days, not just athletes. We as Christians, though, have the advantage of knowing that no matter how bad our day, God is always with us. And He will use those bad days to help us to know Him better.

When you look at it that way, even a golden sombrero can be a good thing in the long run.

........................................

*And we know that God causes everything to work together for the good of those who love God and are called according to his purpose for them.*
ROMANS 8:28 NLT

# GOOFY FOOT

Every sport has athletes who do things a little differently. There are the underhanded free throw shooters in basketball, the sidearm throwers in baseball, the barefoot kickers in football. Even surfers have what some think of as "oddballs"—those who surf with their right foot forward. Most surfers lead with their left.

Surfers—as well as skateboarders, wind-surfers, wakeboarders, and snowboarders—call this the "goofy foot" stance. The origin of the phrase isn't certain, but some believe it comes from a 1937 Disney cartoon. It showed the character Goofy surfing the waves—with his right foot forward.

Whether someone is a goofy foot surfer or a "regular" one depends mostly on which foot is dominant. If someone kicks a football with his right foot, he's probably going to be a "regular" surfer. But if a surfer kicks a football with the left foot, he's probably going to be a goofy foot.

A goofy foot surfer shouldn't try to use a regular stance just to fit in. It's the same way for us as Christians—we should never do things to fit in with unbelievers. God wants believers to live, think, and talk like people who belong to Him, not like people who don't know Him at all.

Nothing goofy about that.

. . . . . . . . . . . . . . . . . . . . . . . . . . . . . . . . . . . . . . . . . . .

*Don't copy the behavior and customs of this world, but let God transform you into a new person by changing the way you think. Then you will learn to know God's will for you, which is good and pleasing and perfect.*
ROMANS 12:2 NLT

# DEKE

If you've ever watched a National Hockey League broadcast on TV, you've probably heard the announcer use the term *deke*. A deke occurs when a player with the puck fakes a move that causes a defensive player to get out of position. Then the offensive player gets an open shot at the goal. The term comes from Canada, and it's a short form of the word *decoy*.

The best goal scorers are the guys who use different kinds of dekes. They know how to fake with their sticks, their heads, their bodies, and even their feet. Sometimes, they change direction or speed. The best dekers are players who use a combination of fakes on a single play, which often ends with the puck in the back of the net.

Dekes are an accepted strategy in hockey, but deception causes all kinds of trouble in other areas of life. The Bible says that the all-time worst deceiver is the devil, who employs every "deke" in his arsenal to fool believers, getting them out of position and missing God's best for their lives.

God doesn't want you to be afraid of the devil, but He does want you to be aware of his deceptive tactics. One day, Satan will be defeated for good. In the meantime, read your Bible to understand—and avoid—the devil's dekes.

. . . . . . . . . . . . . . . . . . . . . . . . . . . . . . . . . . . . . . . . . . .

*"The devil has nothing to do with*
*the truth. There is no truth in him.*
*It is expected of the devil to lie,*
*for he is a liar and the father of lies."*
JOHN 8:44

# GOING IKE

Fans of professional bass fishing know Mike Laconelli for two things: being very good at what he does and his, well, *enthusiastic* reactions when he catches a fish. "Ike" screams, yells, jumps up and down, and pumps his fists every time he gets a bass in his boat. He's developed such a reputation that his fellow professional anglers call a boisterous celebration "Going Ike."

Some of his competitors don't like a lot of Ike's antics. In fact, they find them annoying. But Ike's fans and the people who know him personally will tell you that these celebrations are a picture of "Ike being Ike"—a high-energy, enthusiastic guy who loves fishing, loves competing, and loves celebrating.

Are you the kind of person who jumps up and down and screams when you're happy? If so, great; if not, that's cool too. But the Bible teaches that you can find true happiness in the things you do—whether that's playing sports, working, doing school assignments, or just hanging with your friends—when you act like you're doing them for God Himself.

You can honor God in *everything* you do. The key is to always remember that you're doing those things for your Father in heaven.

. . . . . . . . . . . . . . . . . . . . . . . . . . . . . . . . . . . . . . . .

*Be happy as you work. Do your work as for the Lord, not for men. Remember this, whatever good thing you do, the Lord will pay you for it.*
EPHESIANS 6:7–8

# LAX BRO

In the United States, lacrosse doesn't get the same attention as sports like football, basketball, and baseball. But it still has a lot of players and fans, people who have made the game's culture a part of their lives.

Lacrosse is a unique game played by unique individuals who have their own unique way of interacting. When two lacrosse players meet for the first time, they may refer to each other as a "lax bro"—short for "lacrosse brother."

That's similar to the culture we belong to as Christians. In the New Testament, believers are called names such as "the brethren," "brothers and sisters," and "the church." (Note: that last term isn't just the place where you meet on Sundays, but all the people everywhere who have put their faith in Jesus Christ.)

If you were to read through the whole New

Testament, you might notice the phrase "one another" appearing many times. Jesus told His disciples to "love one another," and the apostle Paul taught Christians to "honor one another above yourselves," "teach one another," "forgive one another," and "serve one another in love"—just to name a few examples.

When you do that, you show God's love to other Christians. . .and to the rest of the world. Just think of all the good that can come from that, bro.

. . . . . . . . . . . . . . . . . . . . . . . . . . . . . . . . . . . . . . . . . . .

*Do not give up. And as you wait and do not give up, live God-like. As you live God-like, be kind to Christian brothers and love them.*
2 PETER 1:6–7

# SIGNING DAY

For college football fans, National Signing Day is like Christmas and your birthday rolled into one. It's the day when the best high school players in the country sign "letters of intent" to play for the university of their choice. National Signing Day is traditionally held on the first Wednesday in February, but over the past few years, players have been allowed to sign their letters during the early signing period in December.

National Signing Day has become a big deal in the sports world. The internet is filled with sites that track football prospects and predict what college they will choose. And the actual signings are reported like big-time news events.

When a can't-miss prospect signs with your team, it's okay to celebrate like you've just gotten an exciting gift. But God has far better gifts for you, starting with the gift of salvation through Jesus. As wonderful as even that gift is, though, God doesn't stop there.

The Bible is filled with promises of blessing for Christians who simply believe God when He says He will do something for them. You can't always measure those gifts in terms of money, or good health, or even a National Signing Day celebration—but you can always be sure that they are the very best God has for you.

. . . . . . . . . . . . . . . . . . . . . . . . . . . . . . . . . . . . . . .

*Whatever is good and perfect comes to us from God. He is the One Who made all light. He does not change. No shadow is made by His turning.*
JAMES 1:17

# GREEN JACKET

Sports fans know that the teams that win league championships win special awards. Hockey has the Stanley Cup, football the Lombardi Trophy, and basketball the Lawrence O'Brien Trophy. Did you know that golf's best tournament—the Masters, held once a year in Augusta, Georgia—gives the winner a jacket? A green jacket, to be exact.

Since 1949, when Sam Snead won the Masters, each winner of the Masters has received the green jacket, which he gets to keep until the following year's event. It's a huge honor, and every professional golfer dreams of standing in front of his fellow players after the tournament and having the previous year's champion present him with the special sport coat.

Everyone likes being honored for their accomplishments, and there's nothing wrong with that. But the Bible says that one day,

Christians who lived faithfully before God will be given the greatest honor of all time.

When you simply believe God's promises, treat others with love, and tell people about Jesus, He notices and remembers. And one day, when you see Jesus in person, you'll receive rewards directly from Him—you'll even sit with Him on His throne!

There's no better honor than that.

. . . . . . . . . . . . . . . . . . . . . . . . . . . . . . . . . . . . . . . .

*"Look! I stand at the door and knock.
If you hear my voice and open the door, I will
come in, and we will share a meal together
as friends. Those who are victorious will sit
with me on my throne, just as I was victorious
and sat with my Father on his throne."*
REVELATION 3:20–21 NLT

# YELLOW JACKET

College sports fans have a special relationship with their favorite teams' mascots. Ohio State fans love Brutus the Buckeye, Oregon fans love The Duck, Colorado fans love Ralphie the Buffalo, and University of Southern California fans love Tommy Trojan.

Georgia Tech fans, though, get to enjoy twice the love—the school has *two* mascots. One is "Ramblin' Wreck," a nicely restored 1930 Ford Model A Sport Coupe that drives out ahead of the football team when they enter the field at Bobby Dodd Stadium. But Tech also has Buzz, a funny and hyper yellow jacket (as in the insect) that's present at every one of the school's sporting events.

In the early days, sportswriters used several names for Georgia Tech teams. But the fans were often called "Yellow Jackets" because they wore (you guessed it) yellow jackets to the games. In 1905, football coach

John Heisman—the same guy the Heisman Trophy is named for—said he wanted his team to be officially known as the Georgia Tech Yellow Jackets.

Those of us who follow Jesus are called by many names too—*Christians*, *believers*, *saints*, even funny words like *branches* and *sheep*. But Jesus has one particular name for us that is really cool: *friend*. No matter where you are or what you're going through, you have a friend who's always with you, always true, and always full of love.

. . . . . . . . . . . . . . . . . . . . . . . . . . . . . . . . . . . . . . . . .

*"I no longer call you slaves, because*
*a master doesn't confide in his slaves.*
*Now you are my friends, since I have told*
*you everything the Father told me."*
JOHN 15:15 NLT

# HAIL MARY

It's one of the most exciting plays of any sport at any level. When it works, it's remembered for years—even decades—to come. It's the "Hail Mary pass."

Hail Marys happen when a team that needs a touchdown to win throws a long pass into the end zone, hoping one of their receivers can catch it. But they rarely work. Desperate teams try the Hail Mary because they're out of options to score and there is little time left on the clock.

The pass is named after a Catholic prayer. The term became popular after Dallas quarterback Roger Staubach (now a Hall of Famer) threw a desperation fifty-yard touchdown heave to Drew Pearson to give the Cowboys a win in the 1975 NFL playoffs. Staubach later said, "I just closed my eyes and said a Hail Mary."

Some people might call Staubach's

successful pass a miracle. But it's really just a lucky and unusual play in a game. A *real* miracle is when God causes something to happen that isn't physically or humanly possible. And He's done a lot of them!

Do you need something you know won't happen unless God makes it happen? If so, you don't need to throw up a Hail Mary—you get to pray in the name of God's own Son, Jesus.

Why not do that now?

. . . . . . . . . . . . . . . . . . . . . . . . . . . . . . . . . . . . . . . . . .

> *Jesus said, "God can do*
> *things men cannot do."*
> LUKE 18:27

# HALF NELSON

Folkstyle wrestling is the kind you see at the youth, high school, and college levels. Most experienced folkstyle wrestlers and coaches will tell you that the "half nelson" is one of the best holds available. Wrestlers learn the half nelson from the time of their first practice in grade school. When it's done right, it can lead to victory.

In the half nelson, a wrestler starts behind his opponent. He passes one arm under the opponent's arm, and then locks his hand on the back of the opponent's neck. Then the first wrestler tries to turn the other player onto his back. The term "nelson" goes back to the early 1800s, and some believe it's from the British naval commander Horatio Nelson.

The half nelson is a powerful weapon that many of the most successful wrestlers have used. But God has given *you* an even more powerful weapon for life: prayer.

The Bible teaches that prayer is the key to defeating the temptation to do wrong things, and getting the strength to do right. Prayer is also the way we ask God for our needs, whether food, clothing, or health. If you want God to do good things for you, go to Him in prayer, believing that He wants to give you everything you need.

The best thing about prayer? You're not "twisting God's arm"—He loves to hear from His kids!

. . . . . . . . . . . . . . . . . . . . . . . . . . . . . . . . . . . . . . . . . .

*"Because of this, I say to you, whatever you ask for when you pray, have faith that you will receive it. Then you will get it."*
MARK 11:24

# HAT TRICK

Usually, when sports fans throw things onto the playing surface, they can get into a lot of trouble. But at hockey games, there are occasions when throwing stuff on the ice is encouraged.

When a home-team hockey player scores his third goal of the game, fans throw their hats onto the ice to celebrate. A three-goal performance is called a "hat trick"—or a "natural hat trick" if the player scores three goals in a row.

Several stories claim to explain how the hat trick got its name. One story, from the Hockey Hall of Fame, says that a Toronto man of the 1930s promoted his business by offering a new hat to any Maple Leaf player who scored three goals in one game.

It's fun to cheer when a player does something great for your favorite team. It's also fun to be recognized when *you* do something well. Just remember to stay humble, as the Bible teaches.

Your friends and family probably won't throw hats your way when you accomplish something big. You may just get a "Way to go!" or a pat on the back. When others say good things about you, enjoy the recognition. And then give God the credit He deserves.

. . . . . . . . . . . . . . . . . . . . . . . . . . . . . . . . . . . . . . . .

*Let another man praise you, and not your own mouth. Let a stranger, and not your own lips.*
PROVERBS 27:2

# HOT CORNER

During the major league season, ESPN's *Baseball Tonight* includes daily "Web Gems"— outstanding defensive efforts by some of the best players in the game. Most shows include great plays in the "hot corner," which is where the third baseman plays. That's the part of the field where right-handed hitters often hit screaming line drives or bouncers.

In recent years, outstanding third basemen like Kris Bryant, Nolan Arenado, and Manny Machado wow fans with their plays at the hot corner. In the past, Hall of Famer Brooks Robinson, "the Human Vacuum Cleaner," set the standard for handling hot-corner plays that no ordinary defender could even dream of making.

Do you think you could field a ball smoked down the third-base line, then make a good throw to first base for the out? That's occasionally what life demands of us.

Sometimes, life can get as heated as baseball's hot corner. And whether we're cocky or scared, God wants us always to look to Him for our confidence. He gives us the ability to face whatever difficulties we come across. He is always with us.

If you play life's "hot corner" right—by letting God work through you—who knows? Maybe someday you'll appear on His own "Web Gems" show.

. . . . . . . . . . . . . . . . . . . . . . . . . . . . . . . . . . . . . . . . . . . . . .

*Then David said to his son Solomon,*
*"Be strong. Have strength of heart, and do*
*it. Do not be afraid or troubled, for the Lord*
*God, my God, is with you. He will not stop*
*helping you. He will not leave you until all the*
*work of the house of the Lord is finished."*
1 Chronicles 28:20

# FREE HAND

When you watch professional bull riders, you might start to think that those old songs about the hard lives of cowboys are true. Bull riders have to finish an eight-second ride on a powerful animal that twists, leaps, spins, turns on a dime, and is really, *really* angry about having a person on its back. And the bull riders have to do their job while holding on *with just one hand*!

Rules require the cowboy to keep one hand in the air for the full ride. In rodeo-speak, that hand is called the "free hand"—and if it touches the bull or any part of the rider's own body, the cowboy is automatically disqualified. He receives no score, even if he manages to stay on the bull for the full eight seconds.

Professional bull riders know that following the rules carefully makes their job harder—and you may run into situations like that too. But the Bible says you should follow the rules anyway. Life goes better—in the long run—when you pay attention to authority, whether that's your parents, your teachers, or the government.

Doing the right thing might seem risky sometimes. But it helps to remember that you make God happy when you follow His rules. . .even if they seem like the hard thing right at the moment.

. . . . . . . . . . . . . . . . . . . . . . . . . . . . . . . . . . . . . . . .

*Teach your people to obey the leaders of their country. They should be ready to do any good work.*
TITUS 3:1

# ICING

It's exciting when your favorite hockey team has the puck in its own offensive zone. Players buzz around the goal, looking for a great shot. The longer the team keeps the puck in that zone, the more tired and confused the defense becomes—and that increases the chance for scoring a goal.

Sometimes the defense has only one option: to shoot the puck the length of the ice over the other team's goal line. When that happens, game officials call the team for *icing*. Icing is an infraction in hockey, but not the kind that leads to players being sent to the penalty box. After one team ices the puck, the referee brings the puck back to the other team's offensive zone for a face-off. The break in play gives the team playing defense a chance to rest, send in fresh players, and get themselves organized.

Even world-class hockey players need a

break sometimes. We all do! And Jesus promised that we can find rest in Him when we need it. "Come to Me, all of you who work and have heavy loads," He said. "I will give you rest" (Matthew 11:28).

When you feel overwhelmed by the stuff life throws your way, there is a place to take a break—in Jesus, who will never leave you to face difficulties on your own.

. . . . . . . . . . . . . . . . . . . . . . . . . . . . . . . . . . . . . . . .

*My being safe and my honor rest with*
*God. My safe place is in God, the rock*
*of my strength. Trust in Him at all times,*
*O people. Pour out your heart before*
*Him. God is a safe place for us.*
PSALM 62:7–8

# LOVE

Some sports terms sound funny because they mean different things in the rest of life. In tennis, for example, a score of "love" means *nothing*—that is, one player hasn't scored against an opponent.

The term goes way back to the 1300s in France. Here's how many believe it happened: In French, the word *l'oeuf*—which sounds like the English word *love*—means egg. Because a zero on a scoreboard looks very much like an egg, the term "love" came to be used in tennis scoring, as in "Serena Williams leads Caroline Wozniacki, 30-love."

"Love" may be nothing in tennis, but it's *everything* in real life. It's one of the most important words in the Bible—maybe *the* most important. The Word of God tells us that we as Christians must love one another. The Bible says that we are to love other people, even the enemies who do or say bad things to us. And scripture teaches that it was God's love that motivated Him to send Jesus to earth. He would live among the people He'd created, teach and heal and encourage them, then die on the cross so we could all be forgiven of our sins.

When you think about it, love is incredible—no matter what tennis says.

. . . . . . . . . . . . . . . . . . . . . . . . . . . . . . . . . . . . . . . . . .

*See what great love the Father has for us that He would call us His children. And that is what we are.*
1 JOHN 3:1

# MENDOZA LINE

Many retired baseball players are remembered for what they did well. But when people recall Mario Mendoza, it's for what he did very poorly: hitting.

Mendoza finished with a career batting average of just .218, and during five of his nine major league seasons, he hit below .200. He was such a weak hitter that players and broadcasters used his name to describe a batting average of .200 or lower. That was "the Mendoza line."

Even though Mario Mendoza was associated with bad hitting, he was far from a failure in baseball. How else could he play almost 10 years in the major leagues? Actually, Mario Mendoza was known as one of the best shortstops in the game. He is a member of Mexico's Baseball Hall of Fame and is known as *Manos de Seda*—"Silk Hands"—in his home country. After he retired as a player, he worked as a minor league manager and a scout for the Angels. Certainly, Mario Mendoza was more than just a weak bat!

In our Christian lives, God has given us the ability to do certain things well—things that honor Him and help others. You may not be good at everything, but that's okay. Just be like Mario Mendoza and do your best with the skills God gives you.

. . . . . . . . . . . . . . . . . . . . . . . . . . . . . . . . . . . . . . . . .

*God has given each of you a gift.*
*Use it to help each other. This will*
*show God's loving-favor.*
1 PETER 4:10

# DRAFTING

When you hear the word *drafting* used in sports, you probably think of the way professional teams select amateur players to join their organizations. You might hear something like the following on the sports report: "The Dallas Mavericks made a great decision in *drafting* Slovenian Luka Doncic in 2018."

In NASCAR racing, though, "drafting" means something completely different. You know that stock cars travel really fast—over 200 miles per hour when the conditions are right. These cars, which can weigh more than three thousand pounds, are greatly affected by something called "drag"—the force of air traveling along the length of the vehicle. To overcome this drag, drivers often practice "drafting," in which one car follows close behind another. This changes the effects of the air flow, and both cars can travel even faster.

Do you have a friend who helps to reduce the "drag" in your life? Are you that kind of friend? A true friend—someone who is always there for you and helps to pick you up when you fall—is not easy to find.

Not easy, but not impossible. To have a great friend, you'll need to be a great friend—someone who's kind and helpful and generous and forgiving. It may take time, but if you work at being a friend, you'll have friends.

Of course, Christians *always* have a true friend in Jesus, who once told His followers, "I call you friends" (John 15:15). He's always happy for you to follow close behind Him.

. . . . . . . . . . . . . . . . . . . . . . . . . . . . . . . . . . . . . .

*A man who has friends must be a friend, but there is a friend who stays nearer than a brother.*
PROVERBS 18:24

126

# PANCAKE

In football, offensive linemen don't get a lot of glory. Their names are hardly ever mentioned over the public-address system, unless they've committed a foul like a false start or holding.

There are no official statistics for offensive linemen. But the "big uglies" up front like to keep track of one themselves: the "pancake." And no, we're not talking about the enormous number of flapjacks they eat in the pregame breakfast!

A pancake is a block so powerful that the defender is driven flat onto his back—flat as a pancake, that is. The phrase "pancake block" dates back to the 1983–84 college season, when University of Pittsburgh offensive tackle Bill Fralic gained national attention for knocking his opponents flat. Pitt's coaching staff began counting the number of times Fralic registered these blocks, and the school's media relations department joined in the fun, labeling them "pancakes."

Still, offensive linemen usually toil away without getting much attention—and many of us as Christians will too. God gives all of His people important work to do, but it's often the kind of work no one else notices.

Whatever job you have, though, you're still an important part of God's team. Work like an offensive lineman, and don't worry if your family and friends overlook it. God notices, and He won't forget it!

. . . . . . . . . . . . . . . . . . . . . . . . . . . . . . . . . . . . . . . . . .

*Nothing should be done because of pride or thinking about yourself. Think of other people as more important than yourself.*

PHILIPPIANS 2:3

# PELOTON

If you've ever watched a long-distance bicycle race like the Tour de France, you may have noticed that riders often stay close to each other on the open road. Toward the end of the race, the best cyclists break away from the pack to zoom toward the finish line.

There's a name for what the riders do and a reason for why they do it.

The group of riders is called a *peloton*, a French word that can be translated "platoon"—which is a group of soldiers. Riders bunch up in a peloton to save energy for later in the race. In a group like that, each rider has less air drag to deal with, and that makes it easier for them to pedal so far for so long. Different riders take the lead in the pack at different times, since it's the lead rider who faces the greatest air resistance.

Think about that: riders in competition actually help each other for most of a race.

And they do it on purpose!

That type of behavior is an example for us as Christians, in how we should treat each other. The Bible says we should serve one another (Galatians 5:13)—even when that doesn't make sense to us.

Life is a lot like a long-distance bike ride—we'll do better when we pedal together!

. . . . . . . . . . . . . . . . . . . . . . . . . . . . . . . . . . . . . . .

*God always does what is right. He will not forget the work you did to help the Christians and the work you are still doing to help them. This shows your love for Christ.*
HEBREWS 6:10

# TRIPLE-DOUBLE

During the 2017–18 season, Oklahoma City Thunder point guard Russell Westbrook made NBA history when he averaged a triple-double (points, rebounds, and assists) for an entire season—for the second year in a row.

Most of the time, a triple-double is accomplished by recording double figures in points, rebounds, and assists. But some players have achieved a triple-double with other statistics, such as blocked shots or steals.

Players who get triple-doubles are versatile—meaning they use a variety of skills to help their team win. In the Bible, a man named Paul wrote of his own versatility and how God had used it to lead others to Jesus (see 1 Corinthians 9:19–23). Paul, who wrote many of the books in the New Testament, is a good example for you to follow every day.

God put Paul—and He puts all of us—in various places and among various people so that we can share the good news about Jesus. Each of us has our own personality, interests, and life story, and God can use who we are to draw others to Himself.

That is an "assist" they will appreciate forever.

. . . . . . . . . . . . . . . . . . . . . . . . . . . . . . . . . . . . . . . . . . . . .

*I have become like every person so in every way I might lead some to Christ. Everything I do, I do to get the Good News to men. I want to have a part in this work.*
1 CORINTHIANS 9:22–23

# PISTE

Like many sports, snow skiing has a long list of terms that insiders know and understand—and outsiders may find strange. In skiing, a "piste" (pronounced "peest") is a marked or groomed path down a mountain. *Piste* is actually a French word meaning trail or run, but in America, skiers often use the term "on-piste" when using the prepared trail, and "off-piste" for backcountry areas that haven't been groomed.

Backcountry skiing is considered much riskier than skiing on prepared trails. There's a higher risk of getting lost or even encountering avalanches. That's why only the most experienced people try off-piste skiing.

Risks are a part of life, and sometimes we have to push through them. The Bible shows us many people who took risks, but it also tells us that before we do something dangerous, we should make sure it's really what God wants us to do. So if some friends suggest that you join them in something you know is risky, first make sure it's something God approves of.

He may tell you not to go "backcountry"— at least not yet. Instead, God may indicate it's best to stick to the bunny hill for a while, until you're ready for more.

. . . . . . . . . . . . . . . . . . . . . . . . . . . . . . . . . . . . . . . . . . .

*So be careful how you live. Live as men who are wise and not foolish. Make the best use of your time. These are sinful days. Do not be foolish. Understand what the Lord wants you to do.*
EPHESIANS 5:15–17

# LET

In one way, tennis is a game of second chances. . .and third chances. . .and fourth chances. . .and so on. Why? Because of the "let."

A legal tennis serve is one that completely clears the net and lands in the opponent's service box (the rectangular area across from and opposite the server). But when the ball touches the net and *then* lands in the service box, the umpire calls a "let" and allows the server to try again.

According to the rules of tennis, there is no limit on the number of lets in one serve. If the player serves up let after let, he or she is allowed to serve again and again.

One of the great things about God is that He gives us Christians second and third and fourth chances. . .even more if we need them. That is good news for all of us, because we so often do things that don't please God. In fact, we often commit the same sins over and over again. But God is patient, and He doesn't give up on us. As Psalm 86:15 says, "But You, O Lord, are a God full of love and pity. You are slow to anger and rich in loving-kindness and truth."

Aren't you glad for God's "lets," His do-overs when you mess up?

. . . . . . . . . . . . . . . . . . . . . . . . . . . . . . . . . . . . . . . . . . . .

*It is because of the Lord's loving-kindness that we are not destroyed for His loving-pity never ends. It is new every morning. He is so very faithful.*
LAMENTATIONS 3:22–23

# QUICK KICK

Even the newest football fan understands that a team facing fourth down in its own territory will punt, hoping to down the ball deep in the opponent's side of the field. But there are circumstances when an offensive team may choose to punt on second or third down. For example, if the Lions are facing a third and very long down from their own ten-yard line, they may choose a tactic called a "quick kick."

When a team quick kicks, it usually does so with the quarterback lined up about five yards behind the center. When the quarterback receives the snap, he kicks the ball as fast as he can. The play usually catches the defense by surprise, which gives the kicking team a better chance at downing the punt farther downfield.

There are times in life when doing the "normal thing"—what most people expect—just isn't an option. And when you don't know what to do, you might be tempted to do nothing and hope the problem solves itself. That doesn't work in football, and it most likely won't work in your life, either.

In those situations, it's best to check with your Coach—God—and ask Him what to do next. Here's what He says He'll do when you pray for help: "If you do not have wisdom, ask God for it. He is always ready to give it to you and will never say you are wrong for asking" (James 1:5).

He may not call for a quick kick. But He's always pleased with your quick prayers.

. . . . . . . . . . . . . . . . . . . . . . . . . . . . . . . . . . . . . . . . . . .

*There were 200 captains of the sons of Issachar. They understood the times and had much understanding of what Israel should do.*
1 CHRONICLES 12:32

# UPSET

Most sports fans love a good upset—unless it's *their* team that loses when it was expected to win. For many fans, their fondest memories involve big upsets, like the New York Giants beating the previously undefeated New England Patriots in Super Bowl XLII, or when Number 16 seed University of Maryland, Baltimore County bested top-seeded Virginia in the first round of the 2018 NCAA men's basketball tournament.

Some people say that calling a big underdog's win an "upset" started when a racehorse named Upset beat the dominant Man o' War in a 1919 race. But the term actually dates back to at least 1877, when it appeared in a story in the *New York Times*.

No matter when or how the word *upset* made its way into sports jargon, it's a good description of how a sports fan feels if his team loses when it was expected to win. It's disappointing, to say the least!

Have you ever felt upset when something you expected to happen didn't happen? The Bible never promised that we could escape all disappointment. But it does promise that God cares for us, and He always has our best interest in mind when He does what He does.

Really, for us as Christians, there are no "losses"—God can turn even our disappointments into victories (see Romans 8:28).

. . . . . . . . . . . . . . . . . . . . . . . . . . . . . . . . . . . . . . . . . . . . .

*Why are you sad, O my soul? Why have you become troubled within me? Hope in God, for I will yet praise Him, my help and my God.*
PSALM 42:11

# GOAT

When sports fans heard the word *goat* in the past, it usually referred to the player who broke their hearts by making a mistake— dropping an easy pass or fly ball, missing a shot, or committing a turnover—a boo-boo that cost his team the Big Game. Lately, though, the word is appearing in all capital letters—GOAT—and stands for *Greatest Of All Time*.

It's fun to talk (or should we say "argue"?) with your sports-loving friends about who's the greatest player of all time for a particu- lar game. For instance, you might think that LeBron James is basketball's GOAT, but one of your friends says it's Michael Jordan. . .or Magic Johnson. . .or Larry Bird. . .or Kareem Abdul-Jabbar.

The name of any sport's GOAT is always up for some fun conversation. But for Christians, there's no question on the identity of the

Greatest Man Who Ever Lived: it's Jesus! He's the only man who was actually God, who came to earth to teach and preach and set an example, then die for our sins and be raised to life again. He's the one who will come back to earth someday, not as a baby this time but as a powerful king. And He's the one who will rule forever over a world that He restored to its original goodness.

Jesus really is the Greatest Of All Time!

. . . . . . . . . . . . . . . . . . . . . . . . . . . . . . . . . . . . . . . . .

*Christ is the visible image of the invisible God. He existed before anything was created and is supreme over all creation, for through him God created everything in the heavenly realms and on earth. He made the things we can see and the things we can't see—such as thrones, kingdoms, rulers, and authorities in the unseen world. Everything was created through him and for him.*
COLOSSIANS 1:15–16 NLT

# RED CARD

Soccer, like every sport, has a list of rules letting players know ahead of time what they can and can't do on the field. Some violations are fairly mild, but others lead to players receiving "yellow cards." A yellow card is a warning to the player to stop breaking a rule. But if the rule breaking is more serious, then the "red card" might come out.

Soccer players receive red cards for a variety of offenses, including unsportsmanlike play, violent contact, spitting on another player, or intentionally using their hands to deny an opponent an obvious goal-scoring opportunity. And a player gets a red card for receiving two yellow cards!

The red card means the player must leave the game and not return. Even worse for that player's team, he or she cannot be replaced, so the remaining team members must play shorthanded.

Nobody likes to be punished, but the rules must be followed for soccer to be fair and fun for everyone. That's a lot like life.

The Bible teaches that God sometimes punishes us when we get out of line. But when God disciplines us, we can still be happy—because it shows that He loves us. He's concerned about how we think, talk, and live.

So if you ever get a "red card"—when things seem hard and unpleasant in your life—it may be that God is trying to get your attention. Know that He wants to help you fix what is wrong in your life.

. . . . . . . . . . . . . . . . . . . . . . . . . . . . . . . . . . . . . . . . .

*Do not give up when you are punished by God. Be willing to take it, knowing that God is teaching you as a son. Is there a father who does not punish his son sometimes?*
HEBREWS 12:7

# RED ZONE

It's both exciting and nerve-wracking when your favorite football team drives down the field into what is called the "red zone"— the area between the twenty-yard line and the goal line. You know your team could make the plays to score a touchdown, but you also know the defense could step up and stop the drive.

Some think former Washington Redskins coach Joe Gibbs was the first to use the term "red zone" to motivate his team. Others say the phrase was coined by Dave Plati, the longtime sports information director at the University of Colorado.

Either way, when a team makes it to the red zone, the goal is to finish the drive and put points on the scoreboard. If those offensive players can't finish the drive, all the yards they gained do nothing but pad the final game stats.

Can you think of something you've started

but not finished—something you know God wants you to complete? Maybe it's a school project or a job you've volunteered to do at church. Or maybe it's the life God called you to live when He first saved you and made you His own child.

Make sure you always finish well—both in the things God has given you to do and the life He expects you to live!

. . . . . . . . . . . . . . . . . . . . . . . . . . . . . . . . . . . . . . . . . . .

*Therefore, since we are surrounded by such a huge crowd of witnesses to the life of faith, let us strip off every weight that slows us down, especially the sin that so easily trips us up. And let us run with endurance the race God has set before us.*
HEBREWS 12:1 NLT

# REDSHIRT

They work just as hard as the starters. They're required to attend all the practices and team meetings, and they have to keep their grades up too. But they're limited in the amount of game time they get. They're the college "redshirts," first-year players who are saving playing time for the next seasons, when they hope they can become a star. In the meantime, their involvement helps the starters, who need someone to practice against every day.

The origin of *redshirt* isn't certain, but it may have begun decades ago when Warren Alfson, a freshman at the University of Nebraska, received permission to practice but not play for the Cornhusker football team. At practice, Alfson wore a red shirt without a number, and eventually his hard work and commitment paid off—by the time he finished at Nebraska, he was named to two all-conference teams and two All-America teams.

Oh, and he also played a season in the NFL before serving in the United States military during World War II.

If you want to do big things in this life, you'll often have to "redshirt"—to prove yourself in the smaller things first. That's usually the way we grow in jobs, whether the kind that makes us money or the ministries that God allows us to do.

So even if the things you do now seem small and unimportant, do them like you're doing them for God Himself. That will make you a star in His eyes.

. . . . . . . . . . . . . . . . . . . . . . . . . . . . . . . . . . . . . . .

*"His owner said to him, 'You have done well. You are a good and faithful servant. You have been faithful over a few things. I will put many things in your care. Come and share my joy.'"*
MATTHEW 25:23

# GRAYSHIRT

While a redshirt freshman spends his first year in college football mainly just practicing with the team, he does have the benefit of being on scholarship while he develops.

But the "grayshirts" don't even have those benefits. They have to wait until the season is over before they can even practice. In fact, they have to pay their own way to school during the first semester because they don't receive any scholarship money.

College football programs offer the opportunity to grayshirt when they've run out of scholarships but still want a certain player on the team—if coaches believe he can develop into a real contributor. Players who accept the grayshirt deal are willing to wait a whole year before officially becoming part of the team.

Grayshirt players are good examples of patience, a character quality God wants every

Christian to possess. In fact, the Bible says, "The Lord wants to show you kindness. He waits on high to have loving-pity on you. For the Lord is a God of what is right and fair. And good will come to all those who hope in Him" (Isaiah 30:18).

Are you waiting for God to do something great in your life—or in the life of someone you care about? Don't let yourself become impatient. Instead, keep praying, keep trusting. . .and wait for God to act.

. . . . . . . . . . . . . . . . . . . . . . . . . . . . . . . . . . . . . . . . . . . . .

*Rest in the Lord and be willing to wait for Him. Do not trouble yourself when all goes well with the one who carries out his sinful plans.*
PSALM 37:7

# PULLING AN ECKMAN

In drag racing, just three-hundredths of a second can mean the difference between a win and a loss. Drivers do everything they can to gain even the smallest advantage—legal or otherwise.

Back in 1997, Jerry Eckman became the first National Hot Rod Association driver to be suspended indefinitely for breaking the organization's rules against horsepower-boosting nitrous oxide systems. Officials at a meet in Columbus, Ohio, discovered Eckman's cheating when a pressurized gas bottle exploded in his pit area, sending chunks of metal flying. NHRA officials determined that Eckman had not only broken the rules but put spectators and other drivers in danger.

Many fans would say that Eckman wasn't the only driver breaking that rule—he was the only one who was caught. But the "other people are doing it" excuse didn't fly with the NHRA.

It doesn't fly with God, either.

Sometimes, we try to excuse our wrong words and actions by looking at others—even other Christians—and thinking, *Well, they're doing it too! Why not me?*

But God doesn't evaluate anyone based on others' behavior. Each of us is responsible for our own actions, and God calls us to live lives of integrity. No cheating, no excuses.

. . . . . . . . . . . . . . . . . . . . . . . . . . . . . . . . . . . . . . . . . . .

*He who is right in his walk is sure
in his steps, but he who takes the
wrong way will be found out.*
PROVERBS 10:9

# RHUBARB

You might wonder what a sour vegetable used in holiday pies has to do with baseball. Just this: a "rhubarb" is a heated argument between a player or manager and an umpire.

The origin of the term isn't known for certain, but Garry Schumacher, a sportswriter in the 1930s, used it for on-field arguments. They "suggested an untidy mess," he said, "a disheveled tangle of loose ends like the fibers of stewed rhubarb."

You might laugh when you see a good rhubarb between a manager and an umpire. But what you're watching is an outburst of anger that wouldn't be appropriate in any other setting. Managers sometimes fly into a rage and say things a person should never say to another human being.

The Bible speaks about fits of anger—and the things people do and say when they happen—and none of it is good. While anger isn't always wrong in God's eyes, it is danger-ous, so He wants us as Christians to make sure we don't hurt other people when we get mad.

Next time you feel a rhubarb coming on, remember this: the person you're angry with is just as valuable to God as you are.

. . . . . . . . . . . . . . . . . . . . . . . . . . . . . . . . . . . . . . . . . . . . .

*My Christian brothers, you know everyone should listen much and speak little. He should be slow to become angry. A man's anger does not allow him to be right with God.*
JAMES 1:19–20

# RIDING THE PINE

No basketball player at any level likes to sit the bench during a game. Players want to be out on the floor, helping their team to win. Playing is a lot more fun than, well, *not* playing.

A team member who doesn't play much is sometimes said to be "riding the pine." No one is sure where that phrase came from, but it certainly goes back to the time when most benches were made of wood. While players know what "riding the pine" means, they also know they don't want to be the guy or girl who does it.

If you're stuck riding the pine, there are some things you can do about it. You can work even harder at practice, support the players who are on the floor during the game, and stay patient as you await your chance to play. If you do those things, you'll be ready when your name is called.

In life, you might find yourself in situations

where you've worked as hard as other people, but the rewards seem slow in coming. But if you are patient and keep a good attitude, you'll be ready when your opportunity comes. And you'll set a great example of the way your fellow Christians should respond when *they* have to wait.

At some point or another, we'll all ride the pine. Let those times spur you on to hard work and trust in God.

. . . . . . . . . . . . . . . . . . . . . . . . . . . . . . . . . . . . . . . . . . . . . . . .

*Do not let yourselves get tired of doing good. If we do not give up, we will get what is coming to us at the right time.*
GALATIANS 6:9

# RIPOSTE

If the fencing term *riposte* sounds like it's from a language other than English, there's a good reason: it is! The word dates to the early 1700s, when English speakers borrowed it from the French. The French word originally came from an Italian term that means "to answer." And the Italian word began with a Latin verb that literally means "to respond."

In fencing, a riposte is a move in which one competitor fends off (or parries) an attack, then makes an attack of his or her own. It's an important move in fencing, and of course the world's best players are very good at it.

The word *riposte* has another meaning, though. It can be a quick, witty reply to an insult.

If you're a fencer, it's okay to use a riposte against your opponent. But the Bible teaches a better way to respond to those who say bad things about us.

Instead of you saying something unkind to a person who put you down, God wants you to pray for that person. You can ask God to do good things for him or her—including saving their souls through Jesus.

That's the best riposte a Christian can use!

. . . . . . . . . . . . . . . . . . . . . . . . . . . . . . . . . . . . . . . . .

*When someone does something bad to you, do not do the same thing to him. When someone talks about you, do not talk about him. Instead, pray that good will come to him. You were called to do this so you might receive good things from God.*
1 PETER 3:9

# SACK

Other than a forced turnover—an interception or a fumble recovery—few things can throw a wrench into a football team's offense quite like a sack. When defenders sack the quarterback, it often puts the offense in the position of needing a long gain to make a first down and keep its drive going.

Quarterback sacks were not kept as an official NFL statistic until 1982. But the term *sack* dates back to the 1960s, when quarterbacks were terrorized by Deacon Jones and the Los Angeles Rams defensive line—known at the time as "the Fearsome Foursome." Jones told NFL Films, "I gave it some thought and came up with the term 'sack', like, you know, you sack a city. You sack a city, you devastate it."

Even though Deacon Jones never recorded an "official" sack in his playing career, researchers have studied his game tapes and concluded that he would have finished his fourteen-year career with 173½ sacks—third most in NFL history.

That's what you call *impact*!

Just as Deacon Jones made a big impact on the game of football, you can make an impact on the world around you. God didn't save you so that you could just wander merrily through life. He saved you to do good things and bring honor to Him.

How can you make an impact today?

. . . . . . . . . . . . . . . . . . . . . . . . . . . . . . . . . . . . . . . .

*For we are God's masterpiece. He has created us anew in Christ Jesus, so we can do the good things he planned for us long ago.*
EPHESIANS 2:10 NLT

# IN THE SOUP

Surfers love it when they catch a big wave they can ride back to shore. Some waves, called "nugs," are really good—especially the ones that turn over on themselves, forming a tube for the surfer to skim through. Cowabunga!

But experienced surfers *don't* like it when they end up in slow-moving whitewater. When that happens to someone, others might say, "That dude just ended up in the soup!" It's not certain where the phrase came from, but it's a pretty good word picture. "In the soup" is a place surfers don't enjoy nearly as much as a big wave.

Do you ever feel like life has you "in the soup"? If so, you're not alone! Grown-ups might put it this way: "I just feel like I'm in a rut." When you seem to be simply plodding along, when it feels like nothing you've asked God to do for you is happening, don't give up.

Instead, remember that God has promised to do good things for you, even if you have to wait for them. His timing is always best.

Keep waiting and believing, and God will eventually send you your own "nug."

. . . . . . . . . . . . . . . . . . . . . . . . . . . . . . . . . . . . . . . . . . . .

*"Do not remember the things that have happened before. Do not think about the things of the past. See, I will do a new thing. It will begin happening now. Will you not know about it? I will even make a road in the wilderness, and rivers in the desert."*
ISAIAH 43:18–19

# MARSHAL

If you enjoy fishing (or know someone else who does), you've probably heard a few fishy stories—you know, exaggerations about the number and size of fish a person has caught. Even the best fishermen in the world are tempted to tell a fib now and again!

In the Bassmaster Elite Series, the highest level of professional bass fishing, people called "marshals" are posted on each competitor's boat for one reason: to protect the integrity of the competition. Participants can be tempted to use illegal bait and tackle or to be less than honest about the size of the fish they reel in. Sadly, over the years several anglers have been caught cheating.

Someone has defined the word *integrity* as "doing the right thing, even when no one is watching." That's a pretty good description, but it leaves out one important fact: someone is *always* watching—God, who knows our every thought and sees each one of our actions. He wants His children, Christians, to live their lives with integrity.

If you want to please God, make sure you approach every area of your life—school, family, and sports—with an eye toward integrity. It's not always easy to do, but it's always the right choice.

. . . . . . . . . . . . . . . . . . . . . . . . . . . . . . . . . . . . . . . . . . . .

*Then I will know that You are pleased with me, because he who hates me does not win over me. As for me, You hold me up in my honesty. And You set me beside You forever.*
PSALM 41:11–12

# THE GREEK CHURCH

If you've ever gone bowling, you know that nothing ruins your score quite like a split on the first throw of a frame. Even for professional bowlers, a split is bad news. Statistics show that the best bowlers in the world manage to pick up a spare on the famous 7-10 split only once every 145 times.

But the 7-10 split isn't even the hardest one to convert. That honor goes to the 4-6-7-9-10 split, also called "the Greek Church." Pro bowlers don't often face the Greek Church, because they don't typically miss so badly on their first throw. When they do, however, they pick up the spare an average of once every 390 attempts. It's not impossible, but it's close.

The Bible says that nothing is impossible for God, and He will often help people do things they couldn't imagine doing on their own. Jesus once said to His followers, "For sure, I tell you, if you have faith as a mustard seed, you will say to this mountain, 'Move from here to over there,' and it would move over. You will be able to do anything" (Matthew 17:20).

God may ask you to do something that seems impossible—to forgive an insult, to love an enemy, to go someplace scary to tell others about Him. How will you respond?

With faith in God, you'll succeed every time.

. . . . . . . . . . . . . . . . . . . . . . . . . . . . . . . . . . . . . . .

*"O Lord God! See, You have made the heavens and the earth by Your great power and by Your long arm! Nothing is too hard for You!"*
JEREMIAH 32:17

# STEEPLECHASE

Running a 3,000-meter race is difficult. That's about 1.86 miles, and it takes a lot of endurance to run it competitively. But when you add a bunch of obstacles—including a big puddle of water—you have an even harder race to run: the steeplechase.

The first Olympic steeplechase was held in 1900, at the games in Paris, France. But the steeplechase name dates to the 1700s, when Irish men rode their horses from one town's church steeple to the next.

Why would a runner choose a race that's even harder to finish than a regular 3,000-meter event? Steeplechasers would probably tell you that the obstacles make the race more interesting and enjoyable.

While we may not enjoy the obstacles that life places in our path, the Bible says that we can still be happy along the way. Sure, having to get through tough things in our path isn't fun. But we know that God has promised to use them to make us stronger in our faith.

What obstacles are you facing today? Pressures at school? Tensions at home? Loneliness? God will help you through each one—and you'll be better on the other side.

. . . . . . . . . . . . . . . . . . . . . . . . . . . . . . . . . . . . . . . . .

*My Christian brothers, you should be happy when you have all kinds of tests. You know these prove your faith. It helps you not to give up. Learn well how to wait so you will be strong and complete and in need of nothing.*
JAMES 1:2–4

# TECHNICAL FOUL

There are several ways basketball teams or players can earn a technical foul. They can get the "T" for everything from failing to check into a game properly to unsportsmanlike behavior toward one another. Most of the time, though, players get called for arguing with or disrespecting a referee.

At most every level of competition, basketball players are disqualified from the game if they receive two technical fouls—and sometimes, they're thrown out for just one if their behavior was bad enough.

When players are ejected, they can no longer help their team because they have to stay on the bench or in the locker room. All of this because of an outburst of anger on the court!

The Bible has much to say about how we are to respond to those in authority over us. God wants us as Christians to control our tempers and respond respectfully to parents, teachers, church leaders, police officers, and other people in charge.

Life is a lot better (and easier) when we learn to treat the authorities with respect, even when we don't agree with their decisions. Just take a deep breath, smile, and move on— don't get called for a technical foul.

. . . . . . . . . . . . . . . . . . . . . . . . . . . . . . . . . . . . . .

*Everyone must submit to governing authorities. For all authority comes from God, and those in positions of authority have been placed there by God.*

ROMANS 13:1 NLT

# BALK

Some words or phrases in sports just *sound* like a description of doing something wrong—and the baseball term *balk* is one of them. A balk occurs when a pitcher makes an illegal move that can deceive base runners. When an umpire calls a balk, the pitch is canceled and anyone on base is awarded the next base—even if that base is home plate.

Rules about balks were first written into the major league rule book in 1898. Before then, pitchers used all kinds of funny moves to deceive base runners. The pitchers wanted to pick off runners for an easy out.

Today, pitchers are most often called for balks when they start their pitching motion and then stop before they throw the ball. Not finishing what you start is a bad thing to do on the pitching mound, and it's not a good thing in life, either.

When you know God has called you to

some job, it's easy to get the project off to a good start. But you put yourself in a place to receive His blessing when you keep working, keep praying, and keep believing until the job is finished.

. . . . . . . . . . . . . . . . . . . . . . . . . . . . . . . . . . . . . . . . . .

*This is what I think. You had better finish what you started a year ago. You were the first to want to give a gift of money. Now do it with the same strong desires you had when you started.*
2 CORINTHIANS 8:10–11

# TOUCHDOWN

In today's game of football, a team scores a touchdown when it carries the ball over the goal line. There are different ways to do that, but they all count for six points. Any player—from either the offense or the defense—can score a touchdown.

But when football was first getting started, it looked more like the game of rugby. In rugby, players had to "touch down" the ball in the end zone to score, so the name of football's scoring play came into being.

In football today, players must still meet certain conditions to score a touchdown. Those conditions are all in the rule books for the level at which they play—high school, college, or professional. If you want the six points, you have to get them according to the rules.

In God's rule book—the Bible—He gives *us* the conditions we need to meet if we want to receive the blessings He has for us. Remember, God loves you and wants to bless you. If you want to learn your part in receiving good things from God, crack open your Bible and start reading.

. . . . . . . . . . . . . . . . . . . . . . . . . . . . . . . . . . . . . . . . . . . . . .

*God can give you all you need.*
*He will give you more than enough.*
*You will have everything you need for*
*yourselves. And you will have enough*
*left over to give when there is a need.*
2 CORINTHIANS 9:8

# TURKEY

How much do you know about turkeys—other than that they are the delicious highlight of any Thanksgiving dinner? Well, for one thing, they aren't the brightest creatures in the animal kingdom. Turkeys—the domesticated kind, at least—have forgotten how to fly, can't run very fast, and are a bit on the clumsy side.

It's hard to imagine why a positive sports accomplishment would be called a "turkey." But in bowling slang, that's the name for three strikes in a row. The term probably started around the end of the 1700s, when bowling tournament prizes often included food items such as—you guessed it—turkeys.

The Bible says that Christians who perform good deeds for God and others will receive prizes—make that "rewards"—when they get to heaven. That's partly why Jesus told His followers, "Do not gather together for yourself riches of this earth. They will be eaten by bugs and become rusted. Men can break in and steal them. Gather together riches in heaven where they will not be eaten by bugs or become rusted. Men cannot break in and steal them" (Matthew 6:19–20).

"Riches in heaven"—including eternal life with Jesus Himself. That sounds a million times better than even the best turkey dinner, doesn't it?

. . . . . . . . . . . . . . . . . . . . . . . . . . . . . . . . . . . . . . . . . .

*"See! I am coming soon. I am bringing with Me the reward I will give to everyone for what he has done."*
REVELATION 22:12

# SPIRIT OF THE GAME

When some high school students from Maplewood, New Jersey, created a new game in 1968, they had no way of knowing that 50 years later, millions of people would be playing it, at both the national and international levels.

Ultimate Frisbee looks kind of like football, but it's played with a flying disc. It's a lot like other competitive sports, with one big exception: at most levels of play, there are no referees. The game has rules, but players enforce the rules themselves. If a disagreement arises, they turn to the "Spirit of the Game," which is similar to the Bible's Golden Rule: "Do for other people whatever you would like to have them do for you. This is what the Jewish Law and the early preachers said" (Matthew 7:12).

We as Christians could learn something from Ultimate players—especially from the way they handle conflicts and arguments on the field. By always showing respect and love for one another, we'll find it easier to settle our disagreements.

God knows that we are all imperfect human beings—at least this side of heaven. But He has given us the Bible so that we can know how to treat one another properly. Life is better when we see the Bible as our guide.

. . . . . . . . . . . . . . . . . . . . . . . . . . . . . . . . . . . . . . . . . . .

*Love each other as Christian brothers.*
*Show respect for each other.*
ROMANS 12:10

# UNASSISTED TRIPLE PLAY

Major league baseball has been around for nearly 150 years, and in that time more than 210,000 games have been played. Can you guess how many times an unassisted triple play has happened? Only 15, through the 2023 season.

An unassisted triple play occurs when a player makes all three outs in an inning, by himself, in a single play. There have to be at least two men on base with no outs, and the UTP usually starts when an infielder catches a line drive for the first out. Then the fielder tags out one runner before he can return to his base, and next tags out a second runner who was on his way to the same base.

Most unassisted triple plays are a matter of an infielder being in the right place at the right time—and being ready for anything that might happen.

Some people in the Bible were in the

right place at the right time—that is, wherever God wanted them to be—and saw Him do something miraculous. Think of Moses, who obeyed God when he was told to go to Egypt—and then saw God perform miracle after miracle to release His people from the pharaoh's slavery.

Do you want to see God do amazing things in your life? Just trust Him enough to be where He wants you to be, when He wants you to be there.

. . . . . . . . . . . . . . . . . . . . . . . . . . . . . . . . . . . . . . . . .

*"For I know the plans I have for you," says the LORD. "They are plans for good and not for disaster, to give you a future and a hope."*
JEREMIAH 29:11 NLT

# YAKKER

A pitcher who can throw hard and with accuracy can find great success in major league baseball. Just think of current players like Aroldis Chapman and Noah Syndergaard or past greats such as Nolan Ryan and Randy Johnson.

But a pitcher who can consistently throw a good curveball can be a nightmare to batters. That's because the curve fools hitters, who don't know just where the ball will be when it reaches the plate.

Curveballs have several nicknames, and most of them—like *bender*, *hook*, or *unfair one*—are easy to understand. Curveballs are also called "the deuce" because catchers often call for them by using a two-finger sign. But another term for a curveball—*yakker*—isn't so obvious.

The curveball is sometimes called a yakker because its path to the plate resembles the swooping flight of a bird known as a yawker. That's another name for the Northern flicker, a fairly common bird in North America.

You've probably heard it said that life has a way of throwing curveballs at us. We don't always know what's coming next, or how we'll handle it. But that's okay, since God will take care of us no matter what.

If He could create the yawker (and He did), He can handle our yakkers (and He knows exactly when and where they'll arrive). Our job is simply to trust His leading.

. . . . . . . . . . . . . . . . . . . . . . . . . . . . . . . . . . . . .

*Give all your worries and cares to*
*God, for he cares about you.*
1 PETER 5:7 NLT

# TRIPLE AXEL

At the 2018 Winter Olympics in Pyeong-chang, South Korea, figure skater Mirai Nagasu made history as the first American woman to land a triple axel jump. Only two other women, from other countries, had pulled off an Olympic triple axel before.

The jump is extremely difficult. The skater leaps into the air, then does three and a half tight rotations before landing. Very few women have landed triple axels in any international competition, let alone in the Olympics.

As you might guess, Mirai Nagasu didn't just skate onto the ice in Pyeongchang and decide to do a triple axel. Making a perfect jump in competition demanded countless hours of practice—and many, many failures. But when she fell, she kept getting up and trying again until she got it right.

We have to have that attitude in life too. We'll all fail at times—even in the things that

God has asked us to do. But He promises that when our heart is set on Him, He'll help us back up when we fall. . .and give us the strength we need to carry on.

Like sports, life is filled with moments of discouragement. But you're only a failure when you don't get up after you fall. If you keep at it, with God as your strength, it's only a matter of time until you succeed in what He's given you to do.

· · · · · · · · · · · · · · · · · · · · · · · · · · · · · · · · · · · · · · · ·

*For a man who is right with God falls seven times, and rises again, but the sinful fall in time of trouble.*
PROVERBS 24:16

# POSER

Serious skateboarders can spot a poser from miles away. They're guys who do everything they can to look and sound like real skateboarders. They use the same words skateboarders use. They might even buy expensive boards or wear popular skater's clothes and shoes. But they have never put in the time and effort it takes to learn to skate well.

The word *poser* is used in lots of social situations, and it's never in a positive way. Being called a poser is the same as being called a fake or a phony. Jesus used another word for posers: *hypocrite.*

Ouch!

If you're a Christian, God doesn't want you to be a poser. He doesn't want you simply to repeat the words Christians speak. He doesn't want you to dress nicely and go to church if your heart really isn't in it. God wants His children to live the kind of life Jesus did while He was here on earth. As the Bible writer James—who was probably Jesus' half brother—said, "Obey the Word of God. If you hear only and do not act, you are only fooling yourself" (James 1:22).

Always be the real deal.

. . . . . . . . . . . . . . . . . . . . . . . . . . . . . . . . . . . . . . . . . .

*"You are the light of the world—like a city on a hilltop that cannot be hidden. No one lights a lamp and then puts it under a basket. Instead, a lamp is placed on a stand, where it gives light to everyone in the house. In the same way, let your good deeds shine out for all to see, so that everyone will praise your heavenly Father."*
MATTHEW 5:14–16 NLT

# SIXTH MAN

Just about every great NBA team has a strong "sixth man" on its roster. He's not part of the starting five, but the first one off the bench. A sixth man may not get the minutes a starter does, but he makes the most of his time—scoring points, playing defense, zipping passes, rebounding—to give the starters a break and keep his team in the game.

Almost everyone wants to start, but certain players have a knack for coming off the bench and doing what they can to help their team win. That's a tremendous example for us as Christians.

We're all part of a team called the "body of Christ," and God has given each of us certain abilities. We each have our own ways of building up, encouraging, and helping other believers, even if they're the "starters," the people who get more attention.

If you've never thought about your special

skills, why not ask God to make them clear to you? And while you're at it, ask people you respect what they think your God-given talents are.

Once you figure them out, use those gifts to the best of your ability. Whether you're a starter or the "sixth man," both you and others will be blessed.

. . . . . . . . . . . . . . . . . . . . . . . . . . . . . . . . . . . . . . . .

*We all have different gifts that God has given to us by His loving-favor. We are to use them. If someone has the gift of preaching the Good News, he should preach. He should use the faith God has given him.*
ROMANS 12:6

# VICTORY FORMATION

If you've watched much football at all, you've no doubt seen the "victory formation"—also known as the "genuflect offense" or simply "taking a knee." Teams often use this play to run out the clock when they're ahead near the end of a game. It's as simple as the quarterback receiving the center snap and immediately kneeling to end the play.

The victory formation is relatively recent. Here's the history: In a 1978 game, the New York Giants led the Philadelphia Eagles 17–12 with 31 seconds left. The Eagles were out of time-outs, and the Giants had the ball. Game over, right? Not necessarily. New York quarterback Joe Pisarcik took the snap, turned, and attempted to hand off to running back Larry Czonka. But, against all odds, the two players botched the play. Eagles cornerback Herm Edwards scooped up their fumble and raced 26 yards for a game-winning touchdown.

The following week, both the Eagles and Giants developed formations to run out the clock at the end of games. It wasn't long before "taking a knee" spread throughout all levels of football.

The Bible says a day is coming when absolutely everyone will "take a knee" to honor Jesus. Many people will do that happily, since they already know and love Him. Some people—those who resist God now—will be forced to bow.

Let's be part of that first group, and encourage people in the second group to join us in bowing before Jesus now. That will be the real "victory formation"!

. . . . . . . . . . . . . . . . . . . . . . . . . . . . . . . . . . . . . . . . .

*Because of this, God lifted Jesus high above everything else. He gave Him a name that is greater than any other name. So when the name of Jesus is spoken, everyone in heaven and on earth and under the earth will bow down before Him.*
PHILIPPIANS 2:9–10

# MORE GREAT STUFF FOR KIDS

Hey, kids, got a minute? Here's an educational book you'll actually *want* to read! It features 1,000 of the most important words and names of scripture—from Aaron, Abba, and Abomination to Zacchaeus, Zeal, and Zion—in understandable, even fun, language to help you know your Bible better.

Paperback / ISBN 978-1-63609-780-0